contents

from the staff

More than ever, today's weddings are about personal style mixed with treasured traditions. This book includes a wealth of beautiful ideas and a plethora of practical projects that you can incorporate into your special day. No detail has been left out. Gather particulars for beautiful bouquets, get inspired by simple and exquisite favors, and ooh and aah over gorgeous wedding cakes. We hope you'll peruse these pages again and again, gaining new ideas each time. Then sit back, relax, and dream of your day to come.

Inspirations
FOR YOUR SPECIAL DAY

Turn your wedding
fantasy into reality with
these stylish ideas for
creating a perfect day.
See how other brides
incorporated their
personal styles into their
special days and let their
real-life weddings spark
your imagination.

A FAMILY AFFAIR

Held at the family's home in a small Connecticut town, this outdoor wedding was all about family and fun. The pretty pink-and-brown reception took place in a daisy-filled barn and under the stars—a casual, intimate, and unforgettable party for 100 close friends and family members.

Two shades of pink peonies, embellished with small yellow flowers and striped silk ribbon, make up this lush bridal bouquet, *opposite*. Displayed en masse, the ethereal blossoms create a luxurious freshness.

This small, old barn, *above*, was transformed into a warm and welcoming space with the help of wreaths, runners, pots, and topiaries as well as bouquets of peonies and daisies.

Natural vistas provide unparalleled wedding decor.

Rolling green lawns and stately trees provided a lush backdrop for the reception, *opposite*. Cocktail tables outside the barn allowed guests to enjoy the early summer evening while hors d'oeuvres were served.

Daisy topiaries constructed from birch branches planted in plaster graced the entrance to the barn, *above*. A rustic bench topped with a pitcher of wildflowers and a pair of candles created a charming resting spot for the guest book.

Guests dined under a tent on the sprawling lawn, *above right*. On the table holding the seating assignments, pink peonies billowed out of silver-plated julep cups. Four rose-petal carpets made a dramatic statement.

Cocktails and hors d'oeuvres were served in the family's old barn, *right*. Twinkling string lights and dozens of white paper lanterns illuminated the dark space, while daisy wreaths draped with long lengths of tulle framed the entry.

Simple blooms make elegant centerpieces.

Narrow, white-clothed Tuscan-style dinner tables, *opposite*, displayed the wedding color combination—chocolate brown (in the linen runner), pink (in the peony arrangements), and chartreuse (in the menus).

Simple menus, *above*, were printed at home, tucked into each guest's napkin, and placed on silver chargers.

Iced cookies in the shapes of starfish, dragonflies, sea horses, and flowers, *above right*, were tasty favors for guests to take home after the reception. Each treat was wrapped in cellophane and tied with a chartreuse ribbon.

A special table for children's beverages was set up just outside the barn, *right*. Large pickle jars surrounded by peonies and daises were filled with ice and provided a choice of three drinks—punch, iced tea, and lemonade.

POMP & PEARLS

Equal parts elegance and beauty, this fairy-tale celebration reinvents the timeless sophistication of Camelot. To achieve the refined look, the bride cloaked a historic mansion in a monochromatic scheme of creamy white and added layers of iridescent pearls, sparkling silver, and shimmery satin.

Pearl-studded wreaths added color and glamour to the reception site's doors, *opposite*. The wreaths were foam rings wrapped in satin ribbon and then embellished with glued-on crafts-store pearls.

To set off their grand entrance, the couple had the banister of the grand stairwell draped with swags made from satin-ribbon sashes and strands of crafts-store pearls. As an added embellishment, small floral bouquets were clipped onto the rails, *right*.

Silver harmonizes with white and is a gentle alternative to more pretentious gold.

Towering bouquets and candles softened the grand reception area, *opposite*. Floral-adorned candelabras with creamy-white tapers cast a gentle glow on the guest tables. Big-bloom flowers, including lilies and hydrangeas, minimized the number of flowers needed.

As a special keepsake, the bride's mother had the back of an antique love seat embroidered with the couple's new monogram, *above*. The head table's low centerpiece allowed guests and photographers to see the newlyweds easily.

A simple computer-generated monogrammed menu was placed in each guest's napkin, *above right*, which was folded to form a pocket cuff.

Table cards are a classy way to help guests find their seats. The bride created these simple signs, *right*, using purchased tent-fold cards, onto which she hot-glued a vellum sheet printed with the table number and a satin bow.

Stop decorations short of overdone. After all, the best decorations are the bride and groom.

The bride's bouquet was an understated bundle of oversize "trumpet" calla lilies in a corset-style holder, *opposite inset*. A thick ribbon was tightly wrapped around the stems and secured with pearl-top corsage pins.

White roses were huddled between each layer of the tiered cake, *above*, which featured the couple's monogram. Pearls and raw-silk bias tape added interest to the hemline of the wispy table skirt.

Instead of sending guests home with a boxed slice of the groom's cake, this couple opted for a tiny candy-box favor embellished with faux pearls and ribbon, *right*.

BACKYARD IN BLOOM

After celebrating many milestones in her family's backyard, this blushing bride transformed the sentimental spot into a gorgeous setting for her casually elegant wedding ceremony and reception. The lush site and a green-and-purple color scheme created the ambience of a stylish garden party.

Urns overflowing with garden roses, blue curiosa, hydrangea, and bells of Ireland greeted guests as they entered the reception area, *opposite*. The flower arrangements sat atop a fence that separated the ceremony and reception areas.

Folding chairs dressed in fabric covers and tied up with purple sashes awaited guests on a blanket of velvety green grass, *above*. An orchid-hued aisle runner complemented the satin backdrop where the bride and groom exchanged vows.

For the perfect location, to say 'I do,' look no farther than your own backyard.

This bride chose a bouquet made of a simple, natural-looking cluster of ribbon-tied blooms, *top left*. The stems were covered with decorative paper and satin ribbons.

Dressed up with a few lengths of ribbon, a small purple ring pouch, and a coordinating bud, this friendly pup made an adorable ring bearer, *above*.

A quote meaningful to the couple was printed onto the front of their handsome ceremony programs, *right*, held together by purple ribbons tied at the bottom.

For stunning yet inexpensive arrangements, the bride filled glass vases with roses and sweet peas and then glued scrapbooking paper and ribbons to the outsides, *opposite, top right.* The floral displays were hung from shepherd's hooks and tree branches.

Potted escort cards continued the wedding's garden theme, *right.* The "Please Take A Seat" sign and individual cards were printed onto scrapbooking paper using a home computer.

A vintage cart was the ideal place to set out drinks for a toast, *below.* A ribbon-bedecked urn made a delightful holder for a bottle of bubbly on ice. Circles were cut from scrapbooking paper and attached around the base of each flute so guests could write their names on them.

Elevating a trio of charming dotted cakes on stands of varying heights is a fun twist on the classic tiered look, *above*. A silky purple backdrop and a generous sprinkling of purple rose petals created a gorgeous setting for the couple's cake-cutting photos.

The bride and groom's initials served as personal cake toppers, *right*. The monograms were crafted from bent wire with silk flowers hot-glued in place.

Tie ceremony and reception spaces together with a unifying color scheme.

Guests were treated to candy-filled wedding favors, *left*, which sat daintily atop lavender transferware. The gifts were craft boxes covered in green-and-white scrapbooking paper and topped with silk flowers.

For this intimate party, guests were seated at long rectangular tables rather than being divided among several smaller tables, *below*.

OUTDOOR ELEGANCE

A beautiful garden was the backdrop for the start of this couple's life as husband and wife. To make the event personal, the couple dressed the scene in their favorite colors and their newly combined monogram and then treasured each moment with friends and family.

The garden's columns were dressed for this special day with florist's-foam cubes covered with carnations and roses, *opposite*. The columns are hollow in the center so a floral arrangement fit snugly inside.

White tulle swags swooped across the center aisle and over the altar to create a dreamlike setting for the ceremony, *above*. The swags were made using metal drapery rods with decorative finials on the top.

A celebration in white, the bridal bouquet featured a lush cascade of calla lilies, roses, tulips, freesia, dendrodium orchids, and lilies-of-the-valley, *above right*.

Guests were given cones filled with rose petals, *right*, which were tossed in the air during the bride and groom's grand send-off. For the instructions, see page 85.

Rose-petal initials on the lawn, *opposite*, added color to the ceremony and continued the wedding's monogram theme. To create the rosy design, a few petals were plotted on the grass to establish the right shape and size first, and then more petals were used to add fullness.

Relax and treasure your first shared moments of happily ever after.

White flowers provide quiet beauty and textural interest.

Guests at this summer wedding loved these ceremony programs, *above left*, which also functioned as fans. The keepsakes featured the couple's monogram over a diamond-grid motif, created by an artist to mimic the paneled windows of the mansion where the wedding was held. For the instructions, see page 85.

Arrangements of stately gladiolas and white tulips created a happy entrance to each row of chairs at the ceremony, *above right*. The bundles were hand-tied together and attached to the chairs using florist's wire and treated with a French wire-ribbon bow to add color to the aisle.

Mounds of pristine hydrangeas spiked with an abundance of roses, tulips, and freesia filled a footed bowl, *left*, creating a special centerpiece for the head table.

To honor the bride and groom, their chairs were given a unique treatment, *right*. An abundance of coral-color organdy fabric was draped over the chairs and held in place with double-faced satin ribbon. Fresh flower corsages were pinned to the chair backs.

A bountiful banquet of flowers gave instant drama to the reception tables, *below*, which were arranged family-style in long lines. Silver flutes took the explosion of flowers above the heads of the seated guests.

Ideas
BIG AND SMALL

Make your wedding day as beautiful as you wish with these elegant ideas. On the following pages, you'll find amazing examples of invitations, bouquets, place settings, and more—everything you'll need to create a truly romantic and personal experience.

Paper Trail

The invitation is a guest's first glimpse into what the wedding will look and feel like.
Use these important pieces not only to communicate who, what,
when, and where but also to reveal something about the event you are planning.

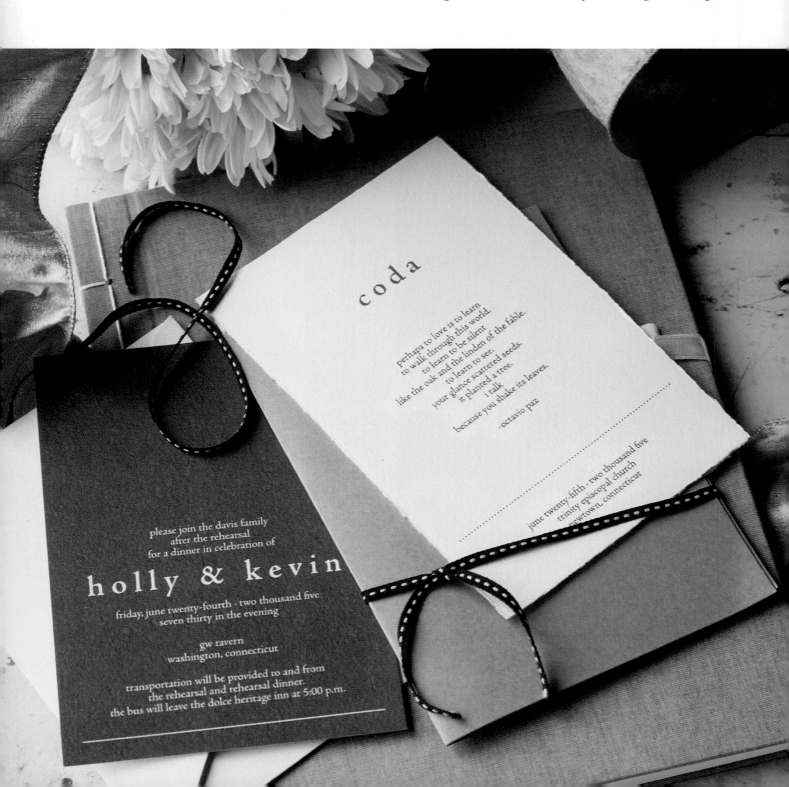

coda

perhaps to love is to learn
to walk through this world.
to learn to be silent
like the oak and the linden of the fable.
to learn to see.
your glance scattered seeds.
it planted a tree.
i talk
because you shake its leaves.

—octavio paz

june twenty-fifth · two thousand five
trinity episcopal church
newtown, connecticut

please join the davis family
after the rehearsal
for a dinner in celebration of

holly & kevin

friday, june twenty-fourth · two thousand five
seven thirty in the evening

gw tavern
washington, connecticut

transportation will be provided to and from
the rehearsal and rehearsal dinner.
the bus will leave the dolce heritage inn at 5:00 p.m.

Printed on ivory card stock in brown ink and delivered in a textured envelope, this invitation, *opposite*, is spare, sophisticated, and equally masculine and feminine. A coda with a poem, accompanying the invitation, sets a contemplative, romantic tone. The entire package is tied up with coordinating ribbon that furthers the stylish, tailored look.

This gracious invitation, *above left*, gives all the wedding details while providing a hint of the beauty and elegance of the upcoming soiree. Decorated with a handcrafted medallion bearing the couple's initials, the computer-printed invitation looks like a custom card-shop creation. For the instructions, see page 86.

This attractive trio, *above right*, proves that a coordinated, handmade wedding ensemble can be simple and still elegant. The same script font, black-and-white photo, and silver accents are repeated on each piece. For the instructions, see page 85.

INVITATION TIME LINE

Like every other element of your wedding, the invitations require thoughtful planning. Be sure to meet every crucial step by following this prewedding countdown.

—SIX MONTHS: Compile your guest list and gather addresses.

—FOUR MONTHS: Begin making your invitations or place an order for purchased cards.

—THREE MONTHS: Start addressing invitations or hire a calligrapher to do it for you.

—SIX WEEKS: Mail out invitations.

—TWO WEEKS: Give caterer final attendance count.

Love in Bloom

Let these inventive, blossom-filled arrangements
inspire the perfect floral creation to capture your style.

Purple roses add depth and interest to this simple, natural-looking cluster of ribbon-tied blooms, *opposite*. The stems are covered with decorative paper, and satin ribbons are hot-glued to the sides of the paper and at the base of the handle.

You might find most of the eye-catching flowers in this bouquet, *above left*, in your own backyard. A single blue hydrangea globe is circled with lavender freesia blooms and a ring of gray dusty miller; the bunch is bound together with florist's tape. Ribbon wrapped around the stems is pinned to the back of the handle with pearl-top corsage pins.

Delicate lengths of ribbon trailing from this bouquet, *above right*, hint at the sweet blossoms nestled together at the other end. The elegant orb displays lavender double tulips, bluebird roses, pink godetia, and lavender dendrobium orchids, with accents of catmint and Kent beauty oregano.

Breathtaking cattleya orchids framed by a pleated purple ribbon form this delicate bouquet, *right*. The stems are secured in the bouquet holder. Long lengths of ribbon are taped onto the top of the holder, and the entire handle is wrapped in ribbon.

Reminiscent of an arrangement gathered from the garden, this bouquet, *left*, earns its delicate ambience from Evelyn and Abraham Darby garden roses. Coral schizostylis adds body against the soft-shade roses, while sprigs of lily-of-the-valley and white snowberries add hints of foliage. Apricot satin ribbon pulls all the hues together.

The autumnal hues in the plaid douppioni silk ribbon that adorns the bouquet, *below left*, reflect the arrangement's crisp blend of flowers. Generous blossoms of orange and yellow dahlias and fresh green gladiolus keep the palette cheerfully bright. The grouping is balanced with the deeper tones in orange montbretia, cockscomb, clover, and copper Echinacea.

A soothing combination of light green, peach, and yellow makes this bouquet, *below*, a treat for the eyes. Celadon hydrangea clusters and hypericum berries are combined with soft yellow orchids and chrysanthemums and peach roses.

The unusual spherical blooms of craspedia create a sleek, modern bouquet, *right*. A bunch of the yellow globes is surrounded with geranium leaves and bound together with florist's tape. A strip of velvet ribbon is attached to the handle with straight pins, and a single craspedia bloom is hot-glued onto the ribbon to look like a button.

This gorgeous bouquet of cymbidium, *below*, is simple to assemble. The stems are layered at an angle and wrapped with green silk ribbon; the handle is topped with a bow. Beaded trim, which was cut into pieces and wired together, is inserted into the bouquet.

TIP: Store your bouquet in water or in a cool space until the morning of the wedding.

Pink nerine lilies nestled with red cockscomb combine to form a lively bouquet, *foreground*. The stems are gathered into a round shape and then bound with waterproof florist's tape. Red satin ribbon is wrapped around the tape, and pink piqué ribbon is tightly braided over the satin to create the look of a corset.

Pink and white Rosita Vendela roses and snowberries look elegant adorned with shimmering pink ribbon and a rhinestone buckle, *background*. Grouped in a spiral fashion, the stems are bound with florist's tape and the handle is covered with 2-inch-wide satin ribbon. A bow is tied at the top of the handle, and an antique buckle is hot-glued to the ribbon.

WORKING WITH
A FLORAL DESIGNER

To walk down the aisle carrying the bouquet of your dreams, be prepared to explain your vision to your floral designer. Follow these tips to prepare for and anticipate your floral planning:

—Clip examples of color combinations you like, from floral arrangements to clothing ensembles.

—Bring information about the style and color of your dress and those of your attendants.

—Convey what you like and don't like about certain arrangements. Use descriptive words, such as "loose," "domed," "natural," "modern," "dramatic," "fun," or "airy."

—Share with the designer how you want your guests to feel when they see the bouquet.

—Hire someone you trust, someone well recommended, and whose work you love.

TIP: Bouquets are easiest to make when they use only one or two kinds of flowers.

Vintage trim adds sparkle to this bouquet, *above*, of deep red and hot-pink roses accented with hypericum berries. Long lengths of rhinestone trim are wrapped around the satin-covered florist's-foam cone and pinned in place. Sheer ribbons around the top edge finish off the look.

Petite Black Beauty roses, dark pink sweet peas, and flowing ribbon make this bouquet, *right*, look as if it's dancing. The stems are arranged in a spiral and then bound together with florist's tape. Six-inch pieces of wired organza ribbon, folded in half, are tucked into the bouquet, and organza is also wrapped around the handle and pinned in place. Long strands of ribbon are then wired around the handle.

Small Wonders

Honor the women and men who will play an important role on your special day with a pretty corsage or sleek boutonniere.

This corsage gets its sweet scent and rich texture from lavender, snowberries, rosemary, and lamb's-ears, *opposite, top left*. Orchids, faux jewels, and shimmery ribbon give it a glamorous touch.

Wrist corsages are great alternatives to the pin-on corsage. This arrangement of lisianthus, dusty miller, rosemary, and coffee foliage is kept in place with an elastic band, *opposite, bottom left*.

Bells of Ireland, dusty miller, and lisianthus combine in this handheld corsage, *opposite right*, which also features gracefully arching wands of white veronica.

A rich red dahlia is the focal point of this boutonniere, *right top*, which also uses dahlia buds and curled red wire. Dahlias bloom in late summer and early autumn and come in orange, red, gold, and deep pink.

A vintage velvet cutout leaf is the basis of this boutonniere, *far right, top*, which also features hypericum berries and velvet-and-satin ribbon binding. If you can't find vintage pieces, look for unique new finds at a fabrics or crafts store.

Wired cluster beads are interspersed with similar-color hypericum berries in this boutonniere, *right, center*. The stems and wires are wrapped in green ribbon.

Calla lilies are an unusual boutonniere flower. Here, a small one, set off with a bit of palm leaf, makes a bold statement, *right, bottom*. Use two or more pins to anchor large flowers, especially when they lie vertically on the lapel.

An unopened lily bud is a surprise component, allowing hypericum berries and a ribbon flourish to stand out, *far right, bottom*. Attaching the ribbon with multiple pearl-head pins adds a decorative finish.

TIP: Make the groom's boutonniere different from the groomsmen's.

An orange-and-green palette sets a dramatic tone for this outdoor wedding, *opposite*. Adorned with bands of roses, an iron gate makes a picture-perfect backdrop for the bride and groom. An orange silk runner and copper troughs filled with miniature and standard cymbidium orchids add more color.

Dress up rented chairs with a pretty and easy floral arrangement, *left*. These chrysanthemum balls are 3-inch florist's-foam balls wrapped in chicken wire and covered with glued-on blossoms.

A pair of stone columns flanks the large gate that serves as the ceremony backdrop. The pillars are topped with overflowing bouquets of orchids that feature trailing garlands, *below*.

TIP: To cut floral costs, hold your ceremony in a garden setting or choose arrangements that also can be used at the reception.

CHOOSING A CEREMONY SITE

When it comes to choosing a place to hold your wedding, the possibilities are endless—from a church or country club to a yacht or baseball field. To whittle down the choices, start by asking yourself a few important questions.

—Is the site **available** when you need it?

—Can the facility **accommodate** all your guests? Is parking available nearby?

—Does the site have any **restrictions** on decorations, music, or photography?

—How much does it **cost**?

—Are **decorating** services provided?

—Who is responsible for **cleaning up**?

—At a beach, park, backyard, or other site without facilities, how much will it **cost to rent** chairs, tents, portable toilets, and other necessities?

—If you are considering an outdoor setting, could **weather** be a problem? Does the site have a backup plan in case of inclement weather?

—If you are considering a church other than your own, does the church welcome **nonmembers**? Does it require couples' **counseling**? Do you like the **officiant**?

Assigned Seating

While escort cards are primarily practical—they guide guests to their tables—they also offer brides an opportunity to be creative. Have fun creating unique designs that match your wedding's theme and finding interesting ways to display the small signs.

At an outdoor wedding, let nature inspire the decor. To create a wheatgrass-covered table to display escort cards, *opposite*, screw plastic garden edging to a table's edge, use spray glue to adhere moss sheets to the tabletop, and plant the surface with wheatgrass. Start the project early so the grass is tall enough by your wedding day.

Crafted of rich brown scrapbook squares and wrapped in cream paper strips printed with the guests' names, the escort cards *above* are a stylish way to direct people to their tables. The cards are laid out on long lengths of wide brown ribbon. A flip of each card reveals the guest's assigned table.

Turn a concrete or foam garden urn into a stunning display space for escort cards, *right*. Plant a wide-leaf hosta inside, and top the urn with a glass round. Finish the look with a satin bow in a color pulled from the cards. Arrange the tent-fold cards in neat, short rows. For the instructions, see page 88.

Welcome guests to the reception with pretty escort cards that match your theme. These tailored designs, *below*, feature the guest's name and a stamp on a plain white paper, which is glued to striped scrapbook paper. The cards are grouped by table and displayed on vintage serving trays lined with ribbon.

ESCORT CARD 101

Also called seating cards, escort cards help your guests find their tables at a sit-down reception. Whether they are tented cards or tags tied to favors, the cards are grouped together, typically near the entryway. Write each guest's or couple's name and table number on a card (use separate cards for couples with different last names), and arrange the cards in alphabetical order in short rows that can be quickly scanned.

Escort cards are often confused with place cards, which are placed at the guest's exact seat at the table. Both types of cards may be used at formal affairs; escort cards may be used alone, but place cards should be used alone only at small affairs where guests can quickly find their tables.

Finishing Touch

After spending so much time and money making your wedding
picture-perfect, zero in on the details. Rental chairs
are often plain and uninspired; dress them up with these novel ideas.

TRUE LOVE

One truly loved or loving;
one whose love is pledged to another.

Lesli & Russ

June 4th, 2005

Share a message with your guests on a chair-back hanger, *opposite, far left*. Print a favorite quote, love poem, or other sentiment onto white paper; cut out and glue onto colored paper. Punch a hole in each corner and thread a length of coordinated ribbon through; tie the ends in knots.

For a fresh and flirty look, tie on a bunch of fresh flowers, *opposite right*. Tie the blooms with lightweight paper-covered florist's wire; leave tails on the wire to attach the bouquet to the chair back. Finish with a simple bow made from wide, double-faced satin ribbon.

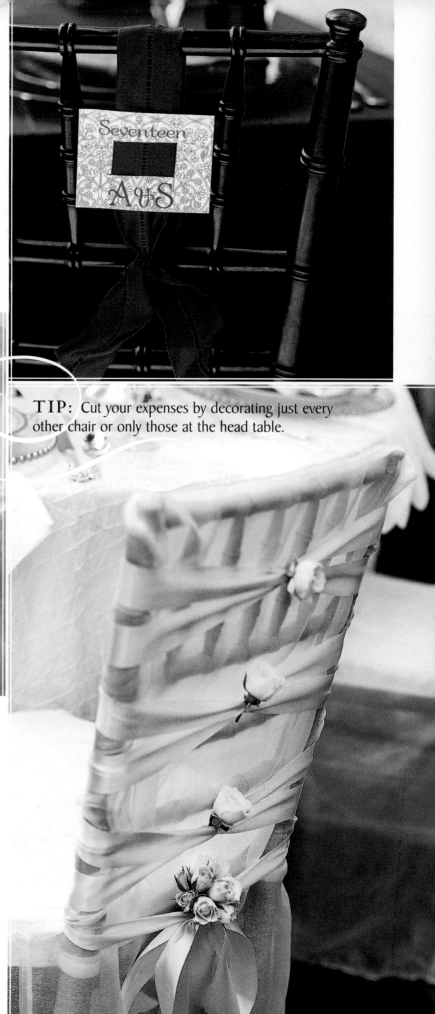

TIP: Cut your expenses by decorating just every other chair or only those at the head table.

A sheer slipcover lends elegance to a plain white chair, *above*. Give each cover personal flair with a simple ribbon, featuring a cluster of silk flowers inserted in the knot. Use wide ribbon when creating chair-back bows; thin ribbons will look too skimpy.

Ribbon adds color and style to simple chairs. This treatment pulls double duty, dressing up the chair and serving as a place card, *top right*. Anchor each numbered card by threading it with wide silk ribbon and tying it to the back of a guest's chair.

Swathed in gossamer, these dreamy chairs nearly look as beautiful as a bridal gown, *right*. The chairs are wrapped corset-style in silk ribbon and finished with fresh flowers. If rental chair covers aren't an option, make your own covers with tulle. It takes about 3 yards to create a flowing drape over a chair.

Set with Style

Wow your guests with beautiful tables. Whether your tabletop decor is elaborate or modest, place settings help set the tone for your party. With just a few easy-to-achieve flourishes, you can turn plain plates into conversation starters.

Menu

Amuse-Bouche
Toasted Brioche Bread Box
Champagne

First Course
Pan-Seared Sea Scallops
Sauvignon Blanc

Second Course
Poached Artichoke Bottom
Chardonnay

Third Course
Tournedo of Beef Tenderloin
Zinfandel

Fourth Course
Roasted Figs
Port

For a casually elegant look, display the evening's menu underneath a clear glass plate at each place setting, *opposite*. Measure the size of the plate well. Size and computer-print the menu onto vellum, and use a circle cutter to cut the menus to fit the plate wells. Punch a hole in the top of each menu, and loop a 12-inch-long ribbon through each hole.

Welcome guests to their tables with a printed menu that matches other wedding stationery, *above left*. Insert the menu and a napkin into a crisp cuff, inspired by a tailored shirt. For the instructions, see page 88.

A pear-topped rosette is a simple, sophisticated accent, *above center*. To create it, gather an 18-inch length of 3-inch-wide double-faced satin ribbon along one long edge using a needle and thread; pull to form the rosette. Let the ribbon tail fall from the center of the plate. Print a name tag or romantic message, and attach it to the stem of each pear.

Let your reception site's architectural elements guide your wedding paper designs. Leaded-glass windowpanes that feature a crosshatch pattern inspired the diamond-grid motif that bands the top of this menu on either side of the monogram, *above right*. For the instructions, see page 88.

For maximum impact, decorate in layers, *right center*. Place a circular menu above center on the top plate and tuck another circle cut from a coordinating paper between the top plate and the charger. Add sparkle to the setting by using a rhinestone belt buckle as a napkin ring.

If you are using a beautiful china pattern, show it off with a simple ribbon treatment, *right bottom*. Cut a length of 2-inch-wide satin ribbon 4 inches longer than the plate. Knot the ribbon near each end and snip the tails into a V shape. Place the ribbon between the china and a clear plate. For trim, tie a sprig of dried lavender with a twist of seam binding.

Deck the Hall

Set the mood for your reception with fabulous centerpieces on each table.
Flower choice, design, and placement will help you
create the perfect atmosphere for your first soiree as a couple.

Making striking flower arrangements is easy with water-absorbing crystals, *opposite*. Fill containers with the crystals and add water; allow the mixture to stand according to the manufacturer's instructions. Tint with food coloring if desired, and then add flowers.

Gorgeous rose balls and painted paper lanterns hang like big ornaments from the trees at this modern reception site, *above left*. Citrus-hued tulips, dahlias, roses, orchids, and chrysanthemums create a zesty atmosphere. Rather than creating one large bouquet for the long tables, several small arrangements are grouped together for greater impact.

These low-lying centerpieces, *above right*, won't interfere with an across-the-table conversation. Moisten a piece of florist's foam so it's wet but not dripping; place the foam on a pedestal. Pin hydrangea leaves around the base; then fill in with hydrangeas, bachelor's buttons, and lilies.

When there's a beautiful backdrop to attract attention, a little goes a long way with decorations. Accent white linens and chairs with simple touches, such as blue flowers and coordinating table runners, *right*.

Finished with a blue satin ribbon, this richly textured arrangement beckons you to admire nature's delicate beauty, *below, inset*. White hydrangeas are tucked into a simple bucket, which is covered with heavy paper printed with a floral pattern. For the instructions, see page 88.

The romantic country charm of garden roses makes them a good choice for a casual outdoor reception, *below*. Create a simple yet stunning centerpiece by loading a silver bucket with the blooms, allowing them to open before the wedding to form big pillows of fragrant petals.

Candles and flowers come together in this romantic-style centerpiece, *opposite left*. Stack a silver bowl atop a silver candelabrum to create a faux epergne that holds bridal-white flowers and candles.

Create an intimate and romantic setting with round tables set with an array of gleaming silver, twinkling candles, and flowers, *opposite, top right*. The shimmering centerpieces reflect the changing light like dewdrops or diamonds.

A magnificent pillar candle encircled by a wreath of full-blown roses and tender rosebuds makes a stunning table decoration, *opposite, bottom right*. Surround the pillar with smaller candles and flower-filled vases. Adorn pristine white candles with pearls to give them a designer touch. For the instructions, see page 89.

TIP: Any watertight container can be turned into a vase.

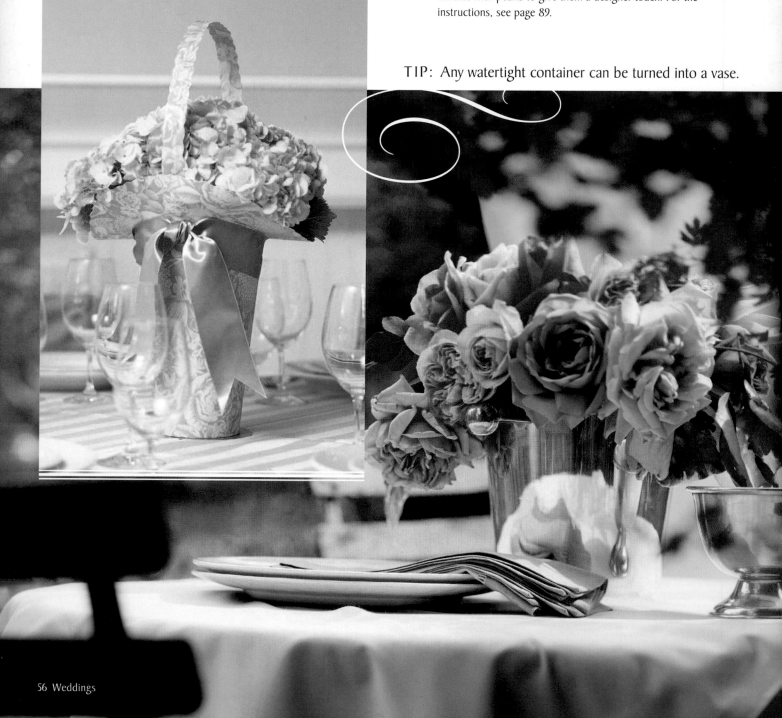

Custom Keepsakes

You'll keep the memories of your wedding forever in your heart. Give your guests
a piece of your cherished day in the form of these handmade keepsakes.
Easily assembled from purchased supplies, they double as dazzling decorations.

Grouped together and tied with ribbon, these paper boxes look like cakes, *opposite*. Display the favors on cake stands of various heights to dress up the cake table. Each "slice" box is filled with blue and white chocolate candies, *left top*. For the instructions, see page 89.

Gift guests with a silk wine caddy that hugs a bottle with warmth and affection, *below and left bottom*. Dress the bag up or down depending on your wedding's style. For the instructions, see page 89.

WEDDING FAVOR TIPS

—Choose your favors based on the location, style, and theme of your wedding. For example, chocolates that could melt may not be wise for an outdoor wedding.

—If you'll be making your own favors, be sure to add the process to your wedding time line. Call on your bridesmaids and family for help.

—Place favors at each guest's place setting, on the escort-card table, or on a table near the reception facility's exit doors.

—Etiquette traditionally calls for giving a favor to each guest. If your chosen gift is on the pricey side, however, it is acceptable to give one favor per couple (just be sure to stick to the one-favor-per-person rule for single guests).

TIP: Consider color and texture as you choose favors for your wedding.

Iced with the bride's and groom's initials, these colorful confections, *opposite top*, appeal to the eye, appetite, and spirit. Based on the concept of friendship necklaces, two heart halves are cut from a single cookie cutter. To master the piped-on initials, practice before lettering the cookies.

Petite layer cakes set on food-safe, bead-edge-glass candle bases are topped with fondant and embellished with flowers, *opposite, bottom left*. The tiny delights are cut from a sheet cake using graduated-size biscuit cutters. For clean edges, freeze the cake and thaw slightly before cutting.

This keepsake heart, *opposite, bottom right*, includes a special quote and is finished with a tassel and ribbon for hanging. To display the favor, hang one on each chair back or create a "favor tree" near the escort-card table. For the instructions, see page 90.

Floral scrapbook papers and coordinating stickers and tags combine to create these pretty favors, *above*. Clear plastic covers the oval window of the favor bag, *left*, making it a delightful way to present flower petals or candies. Treat each guest to a sentimental wedding sound track in a dressed-up CD folder, *right*. For the instructions, see page 89.

Wedding favors date back centuries; original gifts included biscuits, fruits, and nuts.

Sweet-smelling bath salts are pretty and practical favors, *above left*. Dress up a glass bottle with scrapbook paper printed with the bride and groom's names, lavender bath salts, ribbons, lavender rose trims. For the instructions, see page 90.

This lovely favor, *above right*, is easy to make. Wrap French-milled soaps in colorful scrapbook paper, and either tie a simple knot using two or three colors of ribbon or bind it with a straight ribbon topped off with a seal rubber-stamped with the newlyweds' monogram.

Show guests that the bride and the groom are a "perfect pear" with this elegantly wrapped tasty treat, *left*. Gather a circle of tulle around a fresh pear, and tie it with two shades of satin ribbon. Center a wrapped fruit on each guest's plate. Fashion more ribbon across one corner or the edge of the plate to repeat the color.

Toasted Brioche Bread Box
Champagne

Pan-Seared Sea Scallops

Recipes

Tournedo of Beef Tenderloin
Zinfandel

Roasted Figs
Port

Silvery cones filled with heart-shape rice are nestled in a bed of silvered almonds, which provide sparkle and texture, *above left*. Place the bowls of favors near the reception's exit doors. For the instructions, see page 90.

Send guests home with a special reminder of your wedding day—the recipes for your entire menu, *above right*. Layered bands of cream and brown ribbons, along with a brown-and-cream paper monogram, hold each of these recipe envelopes closed. Inside the envelope, a cream-color paper band printed with the word "recipes" holds together the menu and recipe cards for each dish. For the instructions, see page 90.

Present decadent chocolate truffles in champagne flutes wrapped in long lengths of brown ribbon that are tied together at the top, *right*. Let the excess ribbon, also knotted near the ends, drape down the sides. Adhere a paper monogram over one of the ribbon lengths on the side of each glass.

Take the Cake

From an elaborate multitiered concoction to elegant miniature treats,
the wedding cake is a showcase for your personal style.
Get creative with an artfully presented confection that will wow your guests.

This flower-studded cake is nearly too pretty to eat, *opposite and left*. Be sure to have your photographer take lots of pictures before you cut it. This cake begins with a box mix. Then it's enhanced with a luscious lemon or raspberry curd filling tucked under lacy icing. For the recipe, see page 80.

There's nothing more glamorous than an all-white cake. Circled with pleats of ivory chocolate and adorned with ivory-chocolate lilies and ribbon, this four-tier cake, *below left*, is presented on a simple black-stained wood pedestal alongside black-and-white toile-pattern dessert plates for an exquisite tailored look.

Tall and traditional, this beautiful cake, *below right*, befits this happiest of all occasions. The creamy butter frosting is embellished with piped leaves around each tier and a simple vine design on the sides. Fresh flowers add elegance to the edges and top of the cake.

Fancy scroll designs and glossy fondant ribbons make this cake design perfect for an evening wedding, *above left*. Clusters of chocolate-color cosmos, white calla lilies, and fondant ribbons provide additional detail.

Roses and swags shaped from varying shades of butter yellow make this chocolate-wrapped cake glow, *right and above right*. The cake gets its smooth look thanks to a thin layer of butter cream spread over the top and sides of each tier.

Striped-chocolate wraps rendered in shades of olive green and cream give this three-layer cake a thoroughly modern look, *opposite*. The top of each layer is dressed in a different solid color drawn from the palette, and the cake is accented with sweet chocolate roses.

CAKE TRENDS

—Traditional white and chocolate cakes are being joined in great numbers by **more unusual flavors,** such as carrot, red velvet, and piña colada. Fruit filling and champagne frosting also are becoming more popular.

—**Instead of simple roses,** brides now prefer more unusual designs, such as calla lilies and orchids, and often choose real flowers rather than fake or frosted ones.

—**Groom's cakes are back in fashion.** This second, smaller cake is now often a whimsical expression of the groom's hobbies or interests.

—Instead of a traditional cake, many brides are now opting for **a small cake as the centerpiece** of each table, miniature cakes placed at each place setting, or a cupcake tower featuring stacks of cupcakes with different fillings and flavors.

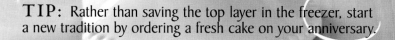

TIP: Rather than saving the top layer in the freezer, start a new tradition by ordering a fresh cake on your anniversary.

You may not be able to take your guests to the Eiffel Tower, but you can bring the charm of Paris to your reception with this memorable cake, *above left*. Trimmed with roses and surrounded by ribbons, the cake is topped with a paper Eiffel Tower. For the recipe, see page 79.

Floor-to-ceiling roses turn a simple cake table into a romantic and dreamy display, *above right*. The chocolate-brown cake with pretty pink detailing echoes the colors of the floral styling, *right*. A lightweight wooden vase with a small display of roses makes a unique cake topper.

Individual servings of champagne-spiked wedding-cake nests stand in for a traditional cake, *opposite, top right*. Each cake is crowned with a coconut nest that holds a white dove, purchased at a crafts store, *opposite, top left*. Instead of using real hydrangeas—which are poisonous—near the food, substitute artificial blooms. For the recipe, see page 79.

The famous robin's-egg blue of a Tiffany's gift box inspired this three-layer box cake, *opposite bottom*, which is wrapped in tinted chocolate. Wavy ribbons show off the sculptural quality of white chocolate, reminiscent of batter lapping into a pan. A scattering of chocolate flowers in pale hues gives the cake a natural look.

TIP: Envision opening the door to the reception and seeing your cake for the first time. What would make you happy?

Crowning Achievements

Give your cake a memorable flourish with a pretty adornment on top.
Whether it's a jeweled brooch or an heirloom design,
a cake topper is a lasting reminder of your special day.

TIP: Whatever your personality or wedding theme, there is a company that can create a topper to suit your needs.

Brides who aren't married to tradition may want to skip the bride-and-groom cake topper in favor of a modern mix of cake-safe flowers and a pretty brooch, *opposite*. Shape, color, and history (not price) makes the piece interesting.

For an alternative to fresh blooms, top your cake with white metal flowers that become treasured keepsakes, *above left*. Rhinestone centers add luster. Because each flower is separate, you can arrange them however you choose.

Make your custom cake more personal with a fashionable monogram topper, *above center*. Be sure the topper you choose is crafted from nontoxic materials. This sleekly styled piece is made of rhodium accented with Swarovski crystals.

Tradition-loving brides appreciate the sentiment of a vintage cake topper, *above right*. Scour thrift shops for an original, or find a replica online. For extra meaning, ask to use your mother's or grandmother's. Add more interest to the topper by adding artfully arranged greenery and black-and-white ribbon.

Perfect for a pair of lovebirds, a fanciful birdcage makes a lovely cake topper, *right*. Here, classic doves get an updated look with rhinestone-dotted flowers. If the topper is heavy, reinforce the cake with dowel rods to prevent it from being crushed.

A Feast for the Eyes

Serve up a delicious treat for your guests with these celebratory menus. Find tasty inspiration with these easy recipes that can help make your culinary dreams come true.
Recipes begin on page 79.

Stone arches draped with giant swags of translucent fabric form a stunning backdrop for a banquet fit for royalty. A pristine table holds towering displays. Each serving dish is filled with an array of delicacies for the guests.

A vase of tender young herbs and fresh green asparagus spears complements an ornate platter of tender-crisp prosciutto-wrapped asparagus, *above*.

Topped with melted cheese, the Gorgonzola crostini, *above right*, must be served in a single layer. Solve space problems by stacking several trays of the bread.

Tender rounds of herb-and-wine flavored marinated pork tenderloin pair perfectly with flaky herb mini biscuits, *right*.

An outdoor venue is the perfect place to celebrate with a flavor-rich menu that includes fresh fruits and vegetables, *opposite*. A variety of coatings makes the shapely breadsticks especially flavorful.

The California Heirloom Insalata, *opposite, inset*, is as beautiful as it is delicious. Several kinds of colorful tomatoes are mixed with fresh mozzarella and flavored with garlic and basil.

This refreshing chilled soup, *left*, gets its kick from fresh ginger and chipotle peppers. For an interesting twist, serve the soup in a petite glass and add a dollop of crème fraiche for smooth creaminess.

Traditionally garlicky aioli gets a zesty twist of lemon in this crabmeat cocktail, *below left*. Black or red caviar and pairs of spiky chive stems garnish the crab cocktail with lemon aioli.

Delicious slices of pork tenderloin are traditional wedding fare. Spice things up for a modern, summer wedding by dressing the meat in a sweet fruit chutney, *below*.

Stunning floral topiaries adorn this buffet table of finger-food appetizers, *opposite*. For mini hors d'oeuvres, serve palmiers (puff pastry pinwheels filled with chopped olives), marinated feta cheese and olives, and purchased mini quiches topped with sour cream.

Unique serving containers lend elegance to easily prepared foods, *above*. Put out baskets of baguettes from your favorite bakery, oodles of olives, and homemade smoked salmon pâté. Serve tarragon-flavored chicken salad on mini croissants.

Easy-to-eat finger foods lend a casual, comfortable feeling to one of the most wonderful days of your life. Decorate food tables with overlays of fabric and tie with extrawide satin ribbon, *above right*.

Topped with fig or plum marmalade and toasted walnuts, warm Brie is a decadent treat, *right*. Serve it with breadsticks, crackers, or toasted baguette slices.

Recipes & Instructions

Take the Cake

BIRD MINI CAKES (*Shown on page 69*)
Makes one 10-inch cake (12 servings) or twelve 4-inch cakes

INGREDIENTS
10-inch fluted tube pan *or*
    twelve 4-inch fluted tube pan molds
1 two-layer-size white cake mix
Champagne
Champagne Icing (see recipe below)
Coconut Frosting (see recipe below)
Shredded coconut
White jelly beans
Purchased dove cake topper(s)

1. Preheat oven to 350°F. Grease and flour a 10-inch fluted tube pan or twelve 4-inch fluted tube pan molds. Set aside.
2. Prepare cake mix according to package directions, substituting champagne for the water. Spoon the batter into the 10-inch pan, or spoon about ½ cup batter into each of the 4-inch molds. (If you have only one pan of 4-inch molds, cover and chill remaining batter while the first batch bakes. Cool, wash, grease, and flour the molds before baking the second batch.)
3. Bake in the preheated oven until a toothpick inserted near the centers comes out clean. (Allow 35 to 40 minutes for the 10-inch pan or 18 to 20 minutes for 4-inch molds.) Cool in pan for 10 minutes. Turn out of pan and cool completely on a wire rack.
4. Place cooled cake(s) on wire rack over waxed paper. Brush **Champagne Icing** over cakes to glaze. Let icing dry.
5. To serve, fill center openings of cake(s) with **Coconut Frosting**. Sprinkle with additional coconut and decorate with white jelly beans and dove(s). Makes one 10-inch cake (12 servings) or twelve 4-inch cakes.

Champagne Icing: In a medium mixing bowl, combine 3 cups sifted powdered sugar, ¼ cup champagne, and ½ teaspoon vanilla. Stir in additional

BIRD MINI CAKES

champagne, 1 teaspoon at a time, to make an icing of glazing consistency. Makes 1 cup.

Coconut Frosting: In a large mixing bowl, beat 1 cup shortening, 1½ teaspoons vanilla, and ½ teaspoon almond extract with an electric mixer on medium speed for 30 seconds. Gradually add 2¼ cups sifted powdered sugar, beating until smooth. Beat in 2 tablespoons milk. Gradually beat in 2¼ cups additional sifted powdered sugar and enough milk (1 to 2 tablespoons more) to make a frosting of spreading consistency. Stir in 2 cups shredded coconut. If desired, tint lightly with blue paste food coloring. Makes 3 cups.

EIFFEL TOWER CAKE (*Shown on page 68*)
This grand tower, excluding the top layer, serves 200.

INGREDIENTS
16×16×2-inch square cake pan
10×10×2-inch square cake pan
6×6×2-inch square cake pan
15 two-layer-size French Vanilla cake mixes
Instant espresso powder
16×16-, 10×10-, and 6×6-inch pieces of
    ¼-inch-thick clear Plexiglas (from a
    hardware store; have it cut to size)
2 recipes Chocolate Filling (see recipe at right)
3 recipes Cream Frosting (see recipe, page 80)
8 white plastic dowels
Large decorating bag fitted with coupler
    and large basket-weave tip
Eiffel Tower cake topper
Edible roses and rose petals

1. Each tier consists of 3 baked cakes. Adding 1 tablespoon espresso powder for each mix, prepare 3 cake mixes for each 16-inch cake (9 mixes total); prepare 2 cake mixes for one 10-inch and one 6-inch cake (6 mixes total).
2. Bake 16-inch cakes, one at a time, in a 325°F oven for 40 to 45 minutes. Bake one 10-inch and one 6-inch cake at the same time according to the package directions.
3. To assemble first tier, stack the three 16-inch cakes on the 16-inch Plexiglas square, spreading **Chocolate Filling** between cakes (use about 6 cups total). Repeat with remaining cakes on Plexiglas pieces, using 2 cups filling for the 10-inch cakes and 1½ cups filling for the 6-inch cakes.
4. Carefully trim the edges of tiers to slant. Using a serrated knife, cut at an angle from about 1 inch from top edge of each tier toward bottom. Do this on all 4 sides of each tier. Use any remaining filling to fill in gaps between cake layers and to thinly cover cut surfaces of cakes. Cover tiers and refrigerate until ready to decorate.
5. To decorate, generously spread sides and top of each tier with **Cream Frosting**. Sides should be as smooth and straight as possible. Insert dowels into the bottom two tiers to support the stacking. Cover tiers and refrigerate until ready to transport.
6. Stack tiers on-site. Pipe angled lines on cake as shown in photo, *page 68*, using **Cream Frosting** and a large basket-weave tip. Pipe all edges of tiers with a zigzag border. Place Eiffel Towel cake topper on cake. Finish decorating the cake with edible roses and rose petals as desired.

Chocolate Filling: In a large mixing bowl, combine 2 cups whipping cream, 2 cups dairy sour cream, 3 cups sifted powdered sugar, and ¾ cup unsweetened European-style cocoa powder. Beat with an electric mixer on medium speed until mixture thickens and holds soft peaks. Makes 6 cups.

Cream Frosting: In a large mixing bowl, combine 16-ounce carton dairy sour cream, 2 cups whipping cream, 2½ cups sifted powdered sugar, and 2 teaspoons clear vanilla or regular vanilla. Beat with an electric mixer on medium speed until mixture thickens and holds soft peaks. Makes 6 cups.

CAKE UNDER CANOPY
(Shown on page 65)
The bottom two layers serve 100 to 130.

INGREDIENTS
2 14×14×2-inch square cake pans
2 10×2-inch round cake pans
2 6×2-inch round cake pans
11 two-layer-size white cake mixes
    10 recipes Creamy White Frosting
    (recipe at right)
Pink paste food coloring
15×15×½-inch wooden board
10-inch round and 6-inch round pieces of
    ¼-inch-thick clear Plexiglas
Purchased lemon or raspberry curd
Large decorating bag fitted with coupler
    and #3, #5, and #12 writing tips
8 white plastic dowels

Fresh Edible Flowers
1. Prepare cake mixes one or two at a time, according to package directions. For the bottom tier, divide 6½ mixes between two 14-inch baking pans (use the remaining batter from ½ mix for cupcakes). For the center tier, divide 3 mixes between two 10-inch round baking pans. For the top tier, divide 1 mix between two 6-inch round baking pans. Bake 14- and 10-inch cakes in a 325°F oven for 55 to 65 minutes; bake 6-inch cakes for 45 to 55 minutes.
2. To decorate the cake, tint 8 recipes **Creamy White Frosting** pale pink; leave 2 recipes of frosting white.
3. To assemble the first tier, stack 14-inch cakes on wooden board, lightly spreading the lemon or raspberry curd between cakes. Repeat with remaining tiers, stacking them on the Plexiglas pieces. Frost tops and sides of all tiers with pink frosting.

4. Mark scallops using the patterns on *page 93*. With a #3 writing tip and white frosting, pipe cornelli lace (meandering unbroken lines) within the marked areas and over the tops of the cakes. Outline the edges of the scallops with a line of dots using a #5 writing tip.
5. Insert plastic dowels into the bottom 2 tiers to support the stacking. Stack the tiers on-site. Pipe a border at the base of each tier using pink frosting and a #12 tip. Decorate the cake with edible fresh flowers as desired.

Creamy White Frosting: In a mixing bowl, beat 1 cup shortening, 1½ teaspoons clear vanilla or regular vanilla, and ½ teaspoon almond extract with an electric mixer on medium speed for 30 seconds. Slowly add 2 cups sifted powdered sugar, beating well. Beat in 2 tablespoons milk. Gradually beat in 2½ cups sifted powdered sugar and 1 to 2 tablespoons milk to reach spreading consistency.
Makes about 3 cups.

A Feast for the Eyes

CRAB COCKTAIL WITH LEMON AIOLI
(Shown on page 75)
Serves 50
If fresh crab is hard to find, look for canned pasteurized crabmeat. A supermarket should be able to order this high-quality product for you.

INGREDIENTS
1½ teaspoons finely shredded lemon peel
⅓ cup lemon juice
2 tablespoons refrigerated or frozen egg
    product, thawed
1 to 2 dashes bottled hot pepper sauce
1 clove garlic, minced (½ teaspoon)
¼ teaspoon salt
⅛ teaspoon ground black pepper
1½ cups olive oil
¾ cup whipping cream
4 pounds cooked dungeness crabmeat,
    coarsely chopped
Caviar
Chive stems

CRAB COCKTAIL WITH LEMON AIOLI

1. For aioli, place the lemon peel, lemon juice, egg product, hot pepper sauce, garlic, salt, and pepper in a food processor or blender. Cover and process or blend until combined. With the processor or blender running, add oil in a thin, steady stream until the mixture is the consistency of mayonnaise. Transfer to a small bowl; cover and chill up to 48 hours.
2. In a chilled large mixing bowl, beat the whipping cream with an electric mixer on medium speed until soft peaks form. Gradually fold the whipped cream into the mayonnaise mixture.
3. To serve, divide crabmeat among 50 small glasses, such as shot glasses. Top each with 1 tablespoon of the whipped cream mixture. Top each with caviar. Garnish with chive stems.

MARINATED PORK TENDERLOIN
(Shown on page 73)
Makes 50 servings
For good browning, avoid crowding the tenderloins in the roasting pan. If your pan is small, roast a few at a time, allowing at least 1 inch between the tenderloins.

INGREDIENTS
6 1-pound pork tenderloins
1 750-milliliter bottle dry white wine
½ cup olive oil
½ cup snipped fresh parsley
¼ cup snipped fresh basil
¼ cup white wine Worcestershire sauce
6 cloves garlic, minced (1 tablespoon)
1 teaspoon cracked black pepper
1 teaspoon salt
Champagne mustard or honey mustard

1. Place pork in two 3-quart rectangular baking dishes. Stir together wine, oil, parsley, basil, Worcestershire sauce, garlic, pepper, and 1 teaspoon salt. Pour over pork. Cover; marinate in the refrigerator up to 24 hours.

2. Preheat oven to 450°F. Drain pork, discarding marinade. Arrange pork on a rack in a large roasting pan. Roast, uncovered, for 30 to 35 minutes or until an instant-read thermometer inserted in center registers 160°F. Cover and let stand for 10 minutes.

3. Transfer tenderloins to a cutting board; thinly slice. Arrange in a storage container. Cover and chill for 4 to 24 hours. To serve, arrange on serving platters. Serve with mustard.

PROSCIUTTO-WRAPPED ASPARAGUS
Makes 100 appetizers (serves 50)
(Shown on page 73)
Buy sliced cheese, or ask the deli to slice it from a large piece; it's almost impossible to cut thin, uniform slices without special equipment. For easier rolling, let the slices stand at room temperature about 15 minutes.

INGREDIENTS
100 asparagus spears (5 pounds), trimmed
    to 6-inch lengths
100 thin slices provolone cheese (4½ pounds)
1¾ pounds thinly sliced prosciutto
2½ cups olive oil
2½ cups balsamic vinegar
2 tablespoons cracked black pepper
Fresh chives (optional)

PROSCIUTTO-WRAPPED ASPARAGUS

1. Place one-fourth of the asparagus spears in a steamer basket. Place in a large skillet with 1 inch boiling water. Cover and steam for 4 minutes. Remove asparagus from steamer basket. Repeat with remaining asparagus, steaming one-fourth at a time.

2. Wrap one cheese slice and one half-slice of prosciutto around each asparagus spear. Arrange spears in two 3-quart rectangular baking dishes. For dressing: in a screw-top jar, combine oil, vinegar, and pepper; shake well to mix. Drizzle half of the dressing over each dish. Cover and chill up to 24 hours.

3. To serve, arrange on a serving platter. If desired, tie a chive around each roll.

GORGONZOLA CROSTINI
(Shown on page 73)
Makes 100 appetizers (serves 50)
Because blue cheeses tend to be on the salty side, use unsalted butter. In many supermarkets, you'll find it in the freezer case.

INGREDIENTS
12 ounces gorgonzola or other blue cheese
½ cup unsalted butter, softened
½ cup finely snipped dried apricots
⅓ cup brandy
100 ¼-inch-thick bias-sliced baguette slices,
    toasted (about two 1-pound baguettes)
¾ cup sliced almonds, toasted (optional)

1. In a large bowl, use a fork to crumble the cheese; add butter. Allow to stand at room temperature for 30 minutes. Mash together cheese and butter with a fork until well combined. Stir in apricots and brandy. Cover and chill cheese mixture up to 24 hours. Allow to stand at room temperature for 30 minutes before spreading.

2. Preheat oven to 400°F. Spread each bread slice with 1 to 2 teaspoons cheese mixture. Place bread slices on baking sheets. Bake for 2 to 3 minutes or until cheese is melted and bubbly. Arrange on serving platters; if desired, top with sliced almonds. Serve crostini at room temperature.

HERBED MINI BISCUITS

HERB MINI BISCUITS *(Shown on page 73)*
Makes about 48 biscuits.
To serve 50: prepare the recipe three times.

INGREDIENTS
4 cups all-purpose flour
2 tablespoons baking powder
½ teaspoon baking soda
1 teaspoon salt
⅔ cup butter
¼ cup finely snipped fresh sage
1½ cups buttermilk
1 egg white
Snipped sage leaves, sesame seeds, and/or
    cracked white pepper

1. Preheat oven to 450°F. In a very large mixing bowl, stir together flour, baking powder, baking soda, and 1 teaspoon salt. Using a pastry blender, cut in butter until mixture resembles coarse crumbs. Stir in ¼ cup snipped sage. Make a well in center of dry mixture. Add buttermilk all at once. Using a fork, stir just until moistened.

2. Turn dough out onto a lightly floured surface. Knead lightly for 10 to 12 strokes. Lightly roll dough into a 15×9-inch rectangle; cut into 1½-inch diamond shapes. Combine egg white and 1 teaspoon water; brush biscuits with mixture and sprinkle with sage, sesame seeds, and/or white pepper. Place biscuits 1 inch apart on large greased baking sheets. Bake in preheated oven for 10 to 12 minutes or until golden.

3. Remove biscuits to a wire rack; cool. Arrange in covered containers; freeze up to 1 month. To serve, thaw at room temperature for 1 hour. Split biscuits and serve on trays.

CALIFORNIA HEIRLOOM INSALATA

CALIFORNIA HEIRLOOM INSALATA

(Shown on page 74)
Serves 50
Bocconcini, small nuggets of fresh mozzarella, are packaged in whey or water. Fresh mozzarella is more delicate-tasting than regular mozzarella.

INGREDIENTS

2 cups olive oil
1 cup balsamic vinegar
12 cloves garlic, minced (2 tablespoons)
1½ teaspoons salt
½ teaspoon ground black pepper
12 to 14 pounds assorted heirloom
    tomatoes, such as Cherokee Purples,
    Green Zebras, and/or Marvel Stripes,
    cored and cut into wedges
2 to 3 pounds mixed baby tomatoes, such
    as sungolds, yellow pear, and/or
    sweet 100s
4 to 5 pounds fresh mozzarella bocconcini
    or fresh mozzarella cheese, cut into
    1-inch pieces
1 cup loosely packed fresh basil shreds
Whole basil leaves

1. For dressing, in a I-quart screw-top jar, combine the oil, vinegar, garlic, salt, and pepper. Cover and chill up to I week. Shake before using.
2. Up to 6 hours before serving, arrange tomato wedges on two to four large platters with rims. Top wedges with the baby tomatoes and mozzarella. Cover and chill. Just before serving, sprinkle platters with the shredded basil and drizzle with dressing. Top with whole basil leaves.

MANGO CAPPUCCINO *(Shown on page 75)*
Makes 4 cups (serves 50)

INGREDIENTS

6 cups seeded, peeled, and coarsely
    chopped mangoes (6 medium) or one
    26-ounce jar refrigerated mango slices,
    drained
1½ cups lime juice
2 tablespoons grated fresh ginger
¾ teaspoon finely chopped chipotle
    peppers in adobo sauce
10 cups orange juice
1½ to 2 teaspoons salt
4 cups Crème Fraiche (see recipe below)
Ground ancho or chipotle chile pepper or
    chili powder

1. Place half of the mango, lime juice, ginger, and chipotle peppers in sauce in a blender or food processor. Cover and blend or process until smooth. Transfer to a very large nonmetallic container. Repeat. Stir together the mango mixtures, orange juice, and salt. Cover and chill overnight or up to 2 days.
2. Serve mango mixture in small stemmed glasses or demitasse cups topped with about I tablespoon **Crème Fraiche**. Sprinkle each serving lightly with ground chile pepper or chili powder. Serve with small spoons.

Crème Fraiche: Beat 2 cups whipping cream and ¼ cup dairy sour cream in a large mixing bowl with an electric mixer on medium speed until soft peaks form. Cover and chill up to 2 hours.

PORK TENDERLOINS WITH FRUIT CHUTNEY

PORK TENDERLOINS WITH FRUIT CHUTNEY *(Shown on page 75)*
Serves 50
Grill the tenderloins the day before the reception. Chill and reheat them unsliced so they don't dry out.

INGREDIENTS

3 tablespoons salt
1 tablespoon sugar
1 tablespoon dry mustard
1 tablespoon ground red pepper
14 ¾- to 1-pound pork tenderloins
3 cups sugar
1½ cups cider vinegar
1½ cups water
3 cups dried cranberries
3 cups golden raisins
1½ cups chopped dried pineapple
1½ cups chopped dried papaya
1½ cups dried apricots cut into thin strips
2 3-inch sticks cinnamon
Halved cherry tomatoes (optional)

1. In a small bowl, stir together the salt, I tablespoon sugar, the mustard, and ground red pepper. Rub salt mixture all over meat. Arrange pork in two large shallow roasting pans. Cover and chill overnight.
2. For chutney, in a 5- to 6-quart Dutch oven, stir together the 3 cups sugar, the vinegar, and water. Bring to boiling, stirring to dissolve sugar. Stir in the dried fruit and cinnamon sticks. Return to boiling; reduce heat. Boil gently, uncovered, until fruit is tender and most of liquid is absorbed, about 40 minutes. Transfer mixture to a large bowl to cool slightly. Serve or cover and chill overnight. (Mixture may be held up to I week in the refrigerator.)
3. For a charcoal grill, arrange medium-hot coals around a drip pan. Test for medium heat above the drip pan. Place meat on the grill rack over the drip pan. Cover and grill for 40 to 50 minutes until an instant-read thermometer inserted in the pork registers 160°F. (For a gas grill, preheat grill. Reduce heat to medium. Adjust for indirect cooking. Place meat on grill rack and grill as above.) Or arrange pork on racks

in large roasting pans, leaving 2 inches between each tenderloin. Roast, uncovered, in a 425°F oven for 25 to 30 minutes or until an instant-read thermometer inserted in pork registers 160°F.

4. Reheat chutney in saucepan over medium-low heat. Slice pork and serve with chutney. If desired, top chutney with halved cherry tomatoes.

To Make Ahead: Wrap grilled, cooled tenderloins unsliced, in foil. Refrigerate overnight. Preheat oven to 300°F. Place foil-wrapped tenderloins in the preheated oven for 40 minutes or until warm.

BREADSTICKS *(Shown on page 74)*
Makes 32 breadsticks
To serve 50: Prepare the recipe twice.

INGREDIENTS
1 cup warm water (105°F to 115°F)
1 teaspoon active dry yeast
1 cup bread flour
1 cup warm water (105°F to 115°F)
5 to 5½ cups bread flour
3 tablespoons olive oil
1½ teaspoons salt
Olive oil
Grated Parmesan cheese
Sesame seeds
Coarse kosher salt and cornmeal

1. In a large mixing bowl, place I cup warm water and sprinkle yeast on the surface; let stand for 5 minutes to soften the yeast. Stir well to dissolve the yeast. Add I cup flour and stir well to make a mix the texture of pancake batter. Let stand at room temperature for I hour.
2. Stir in I cup warm water, 2 cups of the flour, the 3 tablespoons oil, and the 1½ teaspoons salt into the yeast mixture; stir until smooth. Gradually stir in as much of the remaining flour as you can with a wooden spoon. Turn dough out onto a lightly floured surface. Knead in enough of the remaining flour to make a moderately stiff dough that is smooth and elastic (6 to 8 minutes). Divide dough in half.

3. On a lightly floured surface, roll each dough portion into a 10×8-inch rectangle. Cut each rectangle crosswise into sixteen ½×10-inch-long strips. Roll each strip into a 14- to 16-inch-long rope. Brush dough ropes lightly with additional olive oil. Place each coating (Parmesan cheese, sesame seeds, and a mixture of coarse kosher salt and cornmeal) on a separate piece of waxed paper; roll each rope in one of the coatings. Coil one end of each rope. Place breadsticks I inch apart on lightly greased baking sheets. Cover and let rise in a warm place for 30 minutes. Preheat the oven to 375°F.
4. Bake breadsticks for 20 minutes or until bottoms are golden brown and tops are lightly browned. Cool on wire rack. Pack in freezer containers. Seal, label, and freeze to store.

To Make Ahead: Place baked and cooled breadsticks in freezer containers and seal. Freeze for up to 3 months. Thaw at room temperature.

TAPENADE-FILLED PALMIERS
(Shown on page 77)
Makes 80 appetizers (serves 50)
Tapenade is a thick, almost smooth spread made from ripe olives. It's so well seasoned that you don't need any other ingredients in the filling for these savory pinwheel slices.

INGREDIENTS
1 17¼-ounce package (2 sheets) frozen puff pastry, thawed
⅔ cup purchased olive tapenade

1. Line baking sheets with parchment or clean, plain brown paper; set aside. Unfold pastry sheets. On a lightly floured surface, roll one sheet of pastry to a 14×10-inch rectangle. Spread ⅓ cup of the tapenade over the rectangle, spreading to edges. Roll from both short sides to meet in the center. Repeat with remaining dough sheet and tapenade. Cover and chill in freezer about I hour.

TAPENADE-FILLED PALMIERS

2. Preheat oven to 400°F. Trim ends of pastry rolls. Cut the rolls crosswise into ¼-inch-thick slices. Place slices I inch apart on the prepared baking sheets.
3. Bake for 12 to 15 minutes or until golden. Remove and cool on a wire rack. Layer cooled palmiers in a covered container with waxed paper between layers. Cover and freeze up to 3 months. Thaw at room temperature for 30 minutes.
4. Before serving, place slices on a baking sheet. Bake in a 400°F oven for 5 minutes to crispen. Arrange on a serving platter.

TARRAGON CHICKEN SALAD MINI CROISSANTS
(Shown on page 77)
Makes 50 croissants
A ¼-cup ice cream scoop is a quick and convenient tool to ensure exactly the right amount of filling in each mini croissant. You can find scoops of various sizes at department stores and kitchenware shops.

INGREDIENTS
5½ pints purchased deli chicken salad
⅓ to ½ cup snipped fresh tarragon or mint
50 baked miniature croissants (4-inch or smaller), split

In a very large bowl, stir together the chicken salad and the tarragon or mint. Fill each split croissant with about ¼ cup chicken salad mixture. Layer filled croissants in a large roasting pan; cover and chill up to 4 hours. To serve, arrange on serving platters.

MARINATED FETA CHEESE AND OLIVES

(Shown on page 77)

Makes 50 servings

Choose a fairly firm feta cheese and use a sharp, thin-bladed knife to cube it. You can't avoid a bit of crumbling; save the crumbs to top salads and pasta.

INGREDIENTS

1½ pounds feta cheese, cut into 1-inch cubes

2 cups pitted kalamata olives

2 9-ounce packages frozen artichoke hearts, quartered

1 cup olive oil

½ cup lemon juice

¼ cup snipped fresh parsley

2 tablespoons snipped fresh oregano

6 cloves garlic, minced

2 tablespoons dried whole mixed peppercorns, cracked

1. Place cheese cubes in a large bowl. In another large bowl, toss together the olives and artichoke hearts. In a screw-top jar, combine the oil, lemon juice, parsley, oregano, garlic, and peppercorns. Cover and shake well. Divide mixture evenly between the two bowls; toss each gently to coat. Cover and store in the refrigerator for 1 to 2 days.

2. Let mixtures stand at room temperature for 1 hour. Transfer to serving bowl(s). Serve with picks.

SMOKED SALMON PATE

(Shown on page 77)

Makes 7 cups (serves 50)

If you'd prefer a more casual presentation, serve the salmon mixture in one or two bowls or crocks rather than molding it.

INGREDIENTS

3 8-ounce packages cream cheese, cut up and softened

1 cup mayonnaise

⅓ cup sliced green onions

⅓ cup snipped fresh parsley

¼ cup Dijon-style mustard

1¼ pounds smoked salmon, skin removed and broken into chunks

Fresh chives (optional)

Toasted baguette slices

SMOKED SALMON PATE

1. Line 2 bowls with plastic wrap. Combine half of the cream cheese, half of the mayonnaise, half of the green onions, half of the parsley, and half of the mustard in a food processor. Cover and process until smooth. With the processor running, add half of the salmon a few chunks at a time; process until smooth. Pack salmon mixture into a prepared bowl. Repeat with remaining cream cheese, mayonnaise, green onions, parsley, mustard, and salmon; pack into other bowl. Cover and chill up to 24 hours.

2. To serve, unmold pâté onto serving plates. Use a narrow spatula to swirl the surface. Garnish with fresh chives if desired. Serve with toasted baguette slices.

SOUR-CREAM-TOPPED MINI QUICHES

(Shown on page 77)

Makes 100 appetizers (serves 50)

We shopped for cheese mini quiches at a food club and found packages of 60, half flavored with bacon and half flavored with spinach. Use a self-sealing plastic bag with a tip cut off to pipe the dainty sour cream garnish.

INGREDIENTS

100 frozen miniature quiches

1 8-ounce carton dairy sour cream

Small fresh dill sprigs

Arrange quiches on baking sheets and heat according to the package directions. Arrange on serving platters. Top each with about ½ teaspoon sour cream and a dill sprig.

MARMALADE TOPPED BRIE

(Shown on page 77)

Makes 50 servings

To toast the nuts for the topping, spread them in a shallow baking pan and bake in a 350°F oven for 5 to 10 minutes or until light golden brown. Keep an eye on them as they toast, and stir once or twice so they don't burn.

INGREDIENTS

2 20-ounce wheels Brie cheese

3 8-ounce wheels Brie cheese

2 8-ounce jars fig and/or plum jam or preserves

1 cup toasted chopped walnuts and/or almonds

Breadsticks, crackers, or toasted baguette slices

1. Preheat oven to 325°F.

2. Cut off a thin slice from the top of each Brie wheel to remove the rind; discard rind. Place large Brie rounds, cut sides up, on oven-going platters; top with small rounds, cut sides up.

3. Spread tops of wheels with jam and sprinkle with nuts. Bake, uncovered, for 10 to 12 minutes or until Brie is softened and warmed but not runny. Place hot platters on charger plates. Serve with breadsticks, crackers, or toasted baguette slices.

MARMALADE TOPPED BRIE

Outdoor Elegance

PROGRAM FAN AND PETAL CONE

MATERIALS

For all projects:

Card stock and paper: cream and pale blue

Double-faced satin ribbon: ⅝- and
    1-inch-wide

Circle punches: ribbon-stitch; large
    corner rounder; ¹⁄₁₆-, ¼-, and 1¼-inch

Silver spray paint

Bone folder or stylus

Scissors, straightedge, and crafts knife

Adhesives: spray adhesive, crafts glue,
    and tape

Silver thread

For program fan:

1¼×8-inch wood fan handle

For Petal cone:

Scallop-edge scissors

Scoring tool

Monogrammed paper medallion

Paper clip

PROGRAM FAN *(Shown on page 26 and below)*

1. Design the 5¾×7¼-inch fan front, centering a 1⅜-inch-wide border and a 2½-inch-diameter monogram. Plan the program information to fit in a 5¾×7¼-inch area for the fan back. Print the fan front and back on cream card stock and cut out. Round the corners with a large corner rounder.
2. Cut two 6×7½-inch rectangles of pale blue card stock; round the corners with

the corner rounder. Center the printed fan front and back each on a pale blue rectangle with spray adhesive.
3. Paint the wood fan handle with silver spray paint; let dry. Apply spray adhesive to the top 3 inches on one side of the handle, masking off the bottom 5 inches with scrap paper. Center the adhesive side of the handle along the bottom edge on the wrong side of a light blue rectangle; press into place. Spray-mount the second light blue rectangle on the first. Press firmly around all edges. Tie a 23-inch length of 1-inch-wide ribbon into a bow at the front of the handle. Trim the ribbon ends at an angle.

PETAL CONE *(Shown on page 24)*

1. Copy the pattern, *page 91,* onto cream card stock. Cut out the cone using straightedge scissors for the lower ledge edge and scallop-edge scissors for all other edges. Referring to the pattern, lightly score the cone and fold along the dashed lines. Punch a ¹⁄₁₆-inch hole and ribbon-stitch holes in the cone as indicated.
2. Punch a ¹⁄₁₆-inch hole at the top center of a 1¼-inch-diameter medallion. Thread silver thread through the hole in the medallion and knot about 1 inch above the medallion. Insert the thread through the hole in the front flap. Secure the thread with tape on the underside of the flap, positioning the medallion to hang below the bow.
3. Apply a fine line of crafts glue along the long scalloped edge of the underside of the front flap. Fold the cone and secure with paper clips until dry.
4. Thread a 22-inch length of ⅝-inch-wide ribbon through the ribbon holes at the center back of cone and tie into a bow at the front. Cut an inverted V into each end of the ribbon. Secure bow with glue if needed.

Paper Trail

SILVER INVITATION, MENU, AND PROGRAM *(Shown on page 31)*

MATERIALS

Silver card stock

Scissors

Bone folder or stylus

Glue stick

White card stock

Photos

Hole punch

Eyelet and eyelet setter

White vellum

Silver ribbon

1. Use the pattern, *page 92,* to cut the envelope from silver card stock. Score and fold on the dotted lines. Cut a window 1¼-inch below the top edge of the envelope. Adhere the envelope sides and bottom flap together. Use a word-processing program to layout the invitation text within a 4×9⅜-inch space. (You can fit two invitations on one 8½×11-inch sheet.) Make sure to leave a 2-inch square space at the top of the invitation for the photo. Print out the invitations on white card stock and cut them to size. Adhere the photo near the top of the invitation, making sure it can be seen in the window of the envelope.
2. For the menu, print out the text to fit a 4×9⅜-inch space, leaving room at the top of the menu for a photo and an eyelet. Adhere the photo. Center the menu on a larger rectangle of silver card stock and punch a ¼-inch hole at the top through both layers. Set a silver eyelet in the hole.
3. For the wedding program, fold an 8½×11-inch sheet of white card stock and a sheet of white vellum in half widthwise. Lay out all the program pages to fit an 8½×11-inch page horizontally. Print out the pages using the landscape setting, fold them in half, and nest them inside the card stock cover. Adhere a photo to the front of the cover. Layer the folded vellum on top. Cut a piece of silver ribbon twice as tall

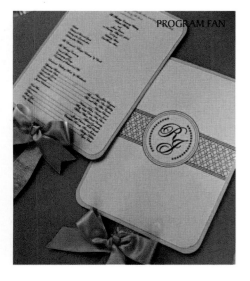

PROGRAM FAN

as the program, plus a little extra for overlap. Center the ribbon on the outside of the program, next to the spine, and adhere the ribbon ends together inside the program, on top of all the pages.

PINK INVITATION AND RSVP CARD

(Shown on page 31 and below)

MATERIALS

Card stock and paper: cream and pale blue

Double-faced satin ribbon: ⅝- and 1-inch-wide

Circle punches: ribbon-stitch; large corner rounder; 1/16-, 1/4-, and 1¼-inch

Silver spray paint

Bone folder or stylus

Scissors, straightedge, and crafts knife

Adhesives: spray adhesive, crafts glue, and tape

Silver thread

1¼-inch-diameter wood, mat board, or paperboard circle

6⅛ × 8⅜-inch cream envelope

3½ × 5½-inch cream envelope

1¼-inch monogrammed paper medallion

INVITATION

1. Planning for the cream card stock to measure 5¾×8 inches, use your computer to create the invitation with a ⅞-inch-wide border ⅞-inch from the top edge. Print the invitation on cream card stock and cut out.

2. Cut a 6×8¼-inch rectangle of pale blue card stock. Center the printed invitation on the pale blue rectangle and adhere with spray adhesive.

3. Spray the wood circle silver. When the paint is dry, mount a 1¼-inch-diameter monogrammed paper

medallion centered on the wood circle with spray adhesive. Center the wood circle on the border with crafts glue. Punch ribbon-stitch holes slightly above the medallion. Thread a 16-inch length of ⅝-inch-wide ribbon through the holes and tie into a bow. Cut an inverted V into each end of the ribbon. Insert invitations into envelopes.

RSVP CARD

1. Planning for the unfolded card to measure 5⅝×6¾ inches, use your computer to center a ⅞-inch-wide border and a 1⅝-inch-diameter monogram on the card front and the response information on the card back inside a 4⅞×3-inch three-line border rectangle.

2. Print the card on cream paper and cut out. Fold the card in half, aligning the 5⅜-inch edges. Crease the fold with a bone folder or stylus. Include a matching RSVP envelope.

Child's Play

SATIN PURSE

(Shown on page 40 and above)

MATERIALS

Tracing paper

Pencil

Compass or ruler

Scissors

¼ yard of lavender silk fabric

¼ yard of thin fleece

Sewing machine

Washable fabrics glue

¾ yard of ⅝-inch-wide lavender braid straight pins

2 yards each of 9/16-inch wide violet and lilac rayon ribbon for handles

Sewing needle and thread

Rubber stamp alphabet set

Ink and inking pad

Lavender card stock

Decorative-edge scissors

⅛-inch hole punch

Four ⅝-inch-diameter antique pewter buttons

SATIN PURSE

1. On tracing paper, draw a half-circle 8½ inches from top to center and 16½ inches on the straight edge (a ½-inch seam allowance is included in the measurement).

2. Use the pattern to cut two half-circles each from fabric and fleece. Fold one fabric shape in half, matching the straight edges. Using a ½-inch seam allowance, stitch along the straight edge, starting at the bottom (tip) and sewing to within 1½ inches of the curved edge. Clip into the seam at the tip; then press the seam open. Using a scant ½-inch seam allowance, baste the fleece to the wrong side of the remaining fabric shape. Assemble as directed for the first shape. Trim the fleece close to the basting line.

3. Slip one cone inside the other with the right sides facing and matching the seam lines. Sew the curved edge, leaving an opening for turning. Clip the curve. Turn the shape right side out and press.

4. Apply fabrics glue to the back of the braid following the manufacturer's directions. Press the braid to the fabric ½ inch from the curved edge, slipping the ends into the opening in the back seam.

5. Slip-stitch the openings closed. Lay the cone flat, with the seam line in the center back.

6. Cut two 32-inch lengths of each ribbon. Holding a light and dark color together, pin two ribbons together 5 inches from each end. Repeat for the remaining two ribbons. Place the pins of one ribbon 1½ inches from each side of the cone; fold and pin in place. Turn the cone over; repeat on the opposite side.

PINK INVITATION AND RSVP CARD

7. Cut two 14-inch lengths each from light and dark ribbon. Holding a light and dark color together, fold the ribbons in half. Hand-gather across the ribbons ¾ inch from the fold. Pull the gathers tightly; then tack the gathers to the tip of the cone.

8. Stamp letters vertically on lavender card stock.

9. Note: The examples in the photo are the French words DOUX ("sweet") and AMOUR ("love"). Cut out in ¾-inch strips, leaving an extra inch of plain paper at the top and bottom. Trim the ends with decorative-edge scissors. Punch a hole in the top of each strip.

10. Secure a threaded needle inside the cone behind a pinned ribbon set. Take the needle to the right side of the cone through the ribbons to secure. Add the stamped strip(s) and a button. Return the needle, taking it through the stamped strip(s) and through the fabric to the inside of the cone. Next, thread the needle through the opposite side of the cone and add a button. Return the needle through the fabric to the inside of the cone. Repeat the threading sequence, knotting the thread on the inside. Always pull the threads taut. Repeat for the opposite side, omitting the stamped strips. Trim the ribbon ends.

PINK CONE *(Shown on page 41)*
MATERIALS
Two 9×16-inch rectangles of wallpaper
Spray adhesive
Tracing paper
Large scallop-edge scissors
Crafts glue
¼-inch hole punch
58-inch length of ½-inch-wide silk ribbon

1. Working on a covered surface, lightly spray the back of a wallpaper rectangle with adhesive. Center and smooth the second wallpaper rectangle onto the adhesive side of the first rectangle. Trace the cone pattern, *page 92*, onto tracing paper and cut out. Trace the pattern onto the layered wallpaper. Use the large scallop-edge scissors to cut on the traced

lines. Fold the basket following dashed lines on the pattern. Overlap the short edges of the container, aligning the fold lines; glue to secure. When the glue is dry, use the hole punch to make a hole centered on each fold of the container about ½ inch from the top edge.

2. From the ribbon, cut three 15-inch lengths for the hanging loop and one 13-inch length for the bow. Align the 15-inch ribbon lengths and knot them together ½ inch from one end. Working from the inside of the container, thread the opposite end of each 15-inch ribbon through one of the holes. Knot the ribbon ends around the hanging loop just above the container. Tie a bow at the center of the 13-inch length of ribbon and glue the bow to the bottom of the container.

WHITE BASKET WITH BUTTON HANDLE
(Shown on page 41 and below)
MATERIALS
Lace doily
Hot-glue gun and hot-glue sticks
Antique hat
Small ivory buttons
2 large ivory buttons
24-gauge wire

1. Hot-glue the doily to the inside of the hat; trim as needed.

2. String assorted small ivory buttons onto the wire to the desired length. String a large button onto each end; twist the large buttons so they will be flat against the inside edge of the hat

WHITE BASKET WITH BUTTON HANDLE

when the handle is placed inside. Trim the wire ends and hot-glue the handle in place.

With This Ring

MONOGRAMMED PILLOW
(Shown on page 42)
MATERIALS
¼ yard of solid-color fabric to match towel
Monogrammed linen tea towel with an embroidered hem
Matching sewing thread
Polyester fiberfill
3½ yards of ⅜-inch-wide double-faced satin ribbon

1. From solid-color fabric, cut two 6½×7½-inch rectangles. With right sides facing, sew the rectangles together with a ¼-inch seam allowance, leaving a small opening on one edge for turning. Clip the corners and turn the pillow right side out. Stuff the pillow with polyester fiberfill. Slip-stitch the opening closed.

2. From the towel, cut two 6½×6¼-inch rectangles using the embroidered hem from the 6½-inch bottom edge and centering the monogram on the front rectangle. With right sides facing, sew the rectangles together on three edges, leaving the embroidered hem edge open. Turn the cover right side out and slip it over the pillow.

3. Cut four 30-inch lengths of ribbon. Tie a four-loop bow at the center of each ribbon length. Sew the center of a bow to each center of the pillow.

HEART-SHAPE PILLOW WITH BROOCH
(Shown on page 43)
MATERIALS
Two antique cocktail napkins or handkerchiefs
Polyester fiberfill
Needle and thread
Satin-center organdy ribbon
Antique brooch

1. Fold one corner of one of the napkins or handkerchiefs toward the center. Beginning at the top of the fold, pinch and gather toward the center to form a heart shape. Repeat with the second napkin or handkerchief. Sew the napkins or handkerchiefs together with right sides facing, leaving an opening along one side.

2. Stuff the pillow with polyester fiberfill through the opening; hand-stitch the opening closed.

3. Form a bow with the ribbon, leaving two long tails. Hand-stitch the bow with the ribbon, leaving two long tails. Hand-stitch the bow to the front of the pillow and pin the brooch on top. Tie the rings onto the long ribbon tails.

Assigned Seating

TENT PLACE CARDS *(Shown on page 49)*
MATERIALS

Card stock and paper: cream and pale blue

Double-faced satin ribbon: ⅝- and
    1-inch-wide

Circle punches: ribbon-stitch; large corner
    rounder; 1/16-, ¼-, and 1¼-inch

Silver spray paint

Bone folder or stylus

Scissors, straightedge, and crafts knife

Adhesives: spray adhesive, crafts glue,
    and tape

Silver thread

1. Planning for the unfolded card to measure 3×2½ inches, use a computer to add the guest's name inside a 3×1¼-inch three-line border rectangle on the card front. Print the card on cream card stock and cut out.

2. Fold the card in half, aligning the 3-inch edges. Crease the fold with a bone folder or stylus.

Set with Style

BLUE CUFF *(Shown on page 53)*
MATERIALS

⅛ yard of blue-and-white striped fabric

⅛ yard of heavyweight interfacing

Two ½-inch-diameter covered-button kits

Note: All measurements include ¼-inch seam allowances unless otherwise noted. Sew with right sides together unless otherwise stated.

1. Cut two cuff pieces from blue-and-white striped fabric and one cuff piece from heavyweight interfacing. Baste the interfacing cuff piece to the wrong side of one blue-and-white stripe cuff piece.

2. Sew the blue-and-white stripe cuff pieces together, leaving a 6-inch-wide opening along the center top of one long straight edge. Trim the corners and seam allowances, and clip the curves. Turn the cuff through the opening; press the raw edges under and slip-stitch the opening closed.

3. Following the button manufacturer's instructions, cover both buttons with blue-and-white stripe fabric. Center and stitch a covered button ½ inch and 1⅛ inches from one cuff end. Sew a centered buttonhole ½ inch from the opposite cuff end. Button the cuff and insert a napkin and menu.

PINK MONOGRAM MENU
(Shown on page 53)
MATERIALS

Card stock and paper: cream and pale blue

Double-faced satin ribbon: ⅝- and
    1-inch-wide

Circle punches: ribbon-stitch; large corner
    rounder; 1/16-, ¼-, and 1¼-inch

Silver spray paint

Bone folder or stylus

Scissors, straightedge, and crafts knife

Adhesives: spray adhesive, crafts glue,
    and tape

Silver thread

1. Design a 3½×8¾-inch menu card with a two-line border on your computer. Position a ¾-inch-wide border 1 inch from the top edge and center a 1¼-inch-diameter monogram on the border with the menu below. Print the menu on cream card stock and cut out.

2. Cut a 3¾×9-inch rectangle of pale blue card stock. Center the printed menu on the pale blue rectangle with spray adhesive.

Deck the Hall

PAPER-COVERED VASE
(Shown on page 56 and below)
MATERIALS:

8-inch-tall galvanized tin bucket

Five 12×12-inch sheets of blue-floral
    scrapbook paper

Spray adhesive

Glue stick

Scallop decorative-edge scissors

Scissors

1 yard of 2-inch-wide blue satin ribbon

Waterproof liner

1. Apply spray adhesive to the outside of the bucket; cover the bucket sides with blue floral scrapbook paper. Cut notches in the paper along the bottom edge of the bucket and fold the notches under to fit. Cut the top edge even with the top edge of the bucket.

2. Use a glue stick to adhere two pieces of blue floral scrapbook paper together with wrong sides facing. Using scallop decorative-edge scissors, cut a 10½-inch-diameter circle to make a collar. Measure the opening of the bucket and cut a circle the same size in the center of the collar using standard scissors. Cut small notches along the center opening. Push the bottom of the bucket through the center opening so the notches fold downward. Push the collar up to the top edge of the bucket. Glue the collar in place along the folded notches; let dry.

3. Wrap the ribbon underneath the collar and tie into a double knot.

PAPER-COVERED VASE

4. Using scallop decorative-edge scissors, cut a 1½×12-inch strip from blue floral scrapbook paper for the handle. Glue the ends to opposite sides of the collar top so the collar bends upward on the sides.
5. Place a waterproof liner inside the bucket; place flowers and water inside.

ROSE-WREATHED PILLAR CANDLE
(*Shown on page 57*)
MATERIALS
Large pillar candle
Florist's-foam wreath
Short-stemmed roses
Long pearl-head pins

1. Soak the wreath in water; and then insert short-stemmed roses, beginning with larger blossoms and filling in the bare spots with rosebuds until the top and outer edges are covered.
2. Secure the wreath to the candle with long pearl-head pins. You will need to use a lot of pins around the top and bottom because the wreath will be quite heavy.
3. Fill in around the candle with more rosebuds if needed.

Custom Keepsakes

CAKE-SLICE FAVOR WHEEL
(*Shown on page 58*)
MATERIALS
Six sheets each of 12×12-inch card stock:
    white and cornflower blue
Crafts knife
Decorative rubber stamp
Blue pigment ink
Glue or double-stick tape
Light blue ½-inch-wide ribbon

1. Trace the pattern, *page 94*, and cut out. Then trace the pattern onto the back of each sheet of white and cornflower blue card stock; cut out. Score along the fold lines using the dull side of a crafts knife.
2. Stamp the box panels with the rubber stamp and blue ink; allow to dry. Fold the box along the scored lines, and use glue or double-stick tape to secure the

sides and bottom of each box. Fill the boxes with desired favor treats.
3. Arrange the cake-slice boxes in a wheel shape atop a platter. Wrap light blue ribbon around the outside of the boxes and tie into a bow; trim the ends at an angle. Add a flower or other small decoration to the top of the favor wheel.

WINE CADDY (*Shown on page 59*)
MATERIALS
Wine or champagne bottle
Shantung silk fabric
Pinking shears
Fabrics glue
Cardboard
Rubber stamps with couple's crest and
    initials
Acrylic paint in desired color
Sponge brush
¾ yard of 1½-inch-wide silk ribbon
    (or width of your choice)
Flower embellishment

1. Measure the height of the wine or champagne bottle; add 6 inches. Find the distance around the bottle, divide this number in half, and add 2 inches. Use these measurements to cut two rectangles of silk fabric with pinking shears.
2. With right sides facing, glue the rectangles together ½ inch from the edges, leaving one short edge open. Press the glued areas firmly with your fingertips to secure. When dry, turn the caddy right side out.
3. Cut cardboard to fit and insert it inside with the sponge brush. Press the stamp onto the front of the wine caddy so the bottom of the image is at least 3 inches from the caddy bottom. Carefully lift the stamp straight off the fabric. Apply paint to the initial stamps and press onto the caddy above the crest. Remove the cardboard when the paint is completely dry.
4. Insert the bottle into the caddy. Fold the excess fabric at the top to the inside. Tie the ribbon around the top; secure a flower in the knot. Cut an inverted V into each end of the ribbon.

FAVOR BAG AND CD FOLDER

To make the favor bag, *above left*, enlarge the template on *page 95* at 200 percent. Trace the pattern onto scrapbook paper, and cut out along the solid lines. Fold the bag along the dotted lines. Overlap the edges, and glue to close.

CD FOLDER (*Shown on page 61 and above right*)
MATERIALS
12×12-inch sheet of scrapbook paper
    embossed with pink roses
12×12-inch sheet of pastel striped
    scrapbook paper
CD folder template, *page 95*
Glue stick
Straightedge and crafts knife
Self-healing cutting mat
Burnisher, stylus, or bone folder
Computer and printer
Stickers: 2 floral frames, 3 flowers,
    2 preprinted die cuts
Foam tape
Cream card stock
Rubber stamps: alphabet
Rubber stamp ink pad: olive
Red seed bead
Temporary adhesive

1. Use a glue stick to adhere the pink roses paper to the pastel striped scrapbook paper with the wrong sides together. Cut out the CD folder template, *page 95*, and enlarge at 200 percent. Trace the template onto one side of the layered scrapbook papers. Using a straightedge and a crafts knife, cut out the folder, including the half-circular tabs, from the layered scrapbook papers.
2. Score the right and left crease lines and fold the flaps in toward the center. Remove the template. Roll the burnisher, stylus, or bone folder over the folder to make the paper lie flat, or crease the folds with a stylus or bone folder.

3. Using your computer, print quotes and messages onto the floral-frame stickers and adhere the stickers inside the flaps. Place the CD in the center of the folder, holding it in place with the tabs. Layer the die-cut stickers using foam tape, and adhere the pair to the bottom of the CD.

4. Cut two 1×6-inch strips from cream card stock. Cut an inverted V into one end of each strip. Use the rubber stamps and ink pad to stamp the bride's and groom's names onto the strips. Layer the three flower stickers using foam tape. Glue the small red seed bead to the center of the top flower. Glue the stamped name ribbons to the back of the layered flower; use temporary adhesive to adhere the assembled flower over the folder closure.

KEEPSAKE HEART *(Shown on page 60)*
MATERIALS
Tracing paper
8½×11-inch sheet each of two coordinating
    scrapbook papers
8½×11-inch sheet of white card stock
Scissors: pinking and medium scallop-edge
Crafts glue
⅛-inch hole punch
1 yard of ¼-inch-wide ribbon
3-inch-long tassel
Transparent tape
Small bunch of flowers
Black calligraphy pen

1. Trace the smaller heart pattern, *page 93,* onto tracing paper, and enlarge 200 percent. Cut it out. Draw around the smaller heart pattern on the back of one sheet of scrapbook paper. Use pinking shears to cut out the heart. Cut a 2×7-inch banner from scrapbook paper. Trim with scallop-edge scissors forming a V shape at the ends.
2. Glue the heart onto the white card stock. Use pinking shears to trim the card stock about ⅜ inch beyond the edges of the scrapbook heart. Use the small hole punch to make a hole below the center top and above the bottom point of the layered heart. Fold one 18-inch length of ribbon in half. Insert

the folded ribbon end through the top hole from the back to the front. Pull the ribbon ends through the folded end.
3. Insert the hanging loop of the tassel through the bottom hole from front to back and tape the loop onto the back. Tie the remaining ribbon in a bow around the top of the tassel. Glue flowers to the bottom of the heart, covering the hole.
4. Use the black pen to write a phrase on the banner. Glue only the banner ends to the heart, allowing the rest to curve.

FAIRY-TALE CONE *(Shown on page 63)*
MATERIALS
12×12-inch sheet of scrapbook paper
Decorative-edge scissors
Glue gun and hotmelt adhesive
7-inch length of 1-inch-wide ribbon
24-inch length of ¼-inch-wide ribbon

1. Using the decorative-edge scissors, cut the scrapbook paper in half diagonally, forming two triangles. Trim the remaining straight edges of each triangle with the scissors. Place the triangles together, wrong sides facing, with the edges slightly off-center to expose the wrong side of the paper at the corners. Hot-glue the triangles together.
2. Overlap the short edges of the triangle to create the desired-size cone; hot-glue in place.
3. Glue the 1-inch-wide ribbon around the center of the cone. Tie the ¼-inch-wide ribbon into a bow, and glue it to the center front of the wider ribbon.

BATH SALTS *(Shown on page 62)*
MATERIALS
Scrapbook paper
Scissors
Rotary cutter, cutting mat, and ruler; or
    paper cutter (optional)
Decorative-edge scissors
Corked glass bottle
Small funnel
Lavender bath salts
8 inches of ½-inch-wide seam-binding
    ribbon (we used Midori ribbon)
Small lilac paper rose found in most crafts
    and scrapbooking stores

1. Using a word-processing program, type the names of the bride and groom repeatedly in a row across your computer screen. Use a font and a size that allow the names to fit comfortably within a ½-inch-high strip. Print the names on scrapbook paper.
2. Cut out the row to measure ½ inch high and 8½ inch long. Retrim the bottom edge using decorative-edge scissors.
3. Coil the strip, print side out, into the bottle. Fill the bottle with bath salts and add the cork stopper.
4. Tie ribbon around the cork and dab with glue at the knot. Place a small lavender rose on the knot. Trim the ends.

RECIPE WEDDING FAVOR
(Shown on page 63)
MATERIALS
2 pieces of 8½×11-inch cream card stock
6×9-inch four-fold envelope in bronze
14-inch length of 2-inch-wide chocolate-
    brown double-faced satin ribbon
14-inch length of 2¾-inch-wide ivory
    double-faced satin ribbon
2×2-inch monogram
Paper cutter
Double-stick tape

1. Using a word-processing program, set up a new document with two columns. Type two recipes side by side and evenly spaced in the font type and size you desire. Using landscape mode, print the recipes onto cream card stock. Trim each recipe to 5½×8½ inches with a paper cutter.
2. Type the word "Recipes" centered in standard letter-size format in the font type and size you desire. Print the word on cream card stock. Trim into a 2½-inch-wide band. Wrap the band around the recipe cards and secure with double-stick tape.
3. Place the wrapped cards inside the envelope and fold in the flaps. Wrap ivory ribbon around the center of the envelope and secure with double-stick tape. Wrap the chocolate-brown ribbon around the ivory ribbon. Center the monogram on top of the ribbons and tape in place.

All patterns are actual size unless otherwise noted.

Dashes indicate lines for folding during assemble.

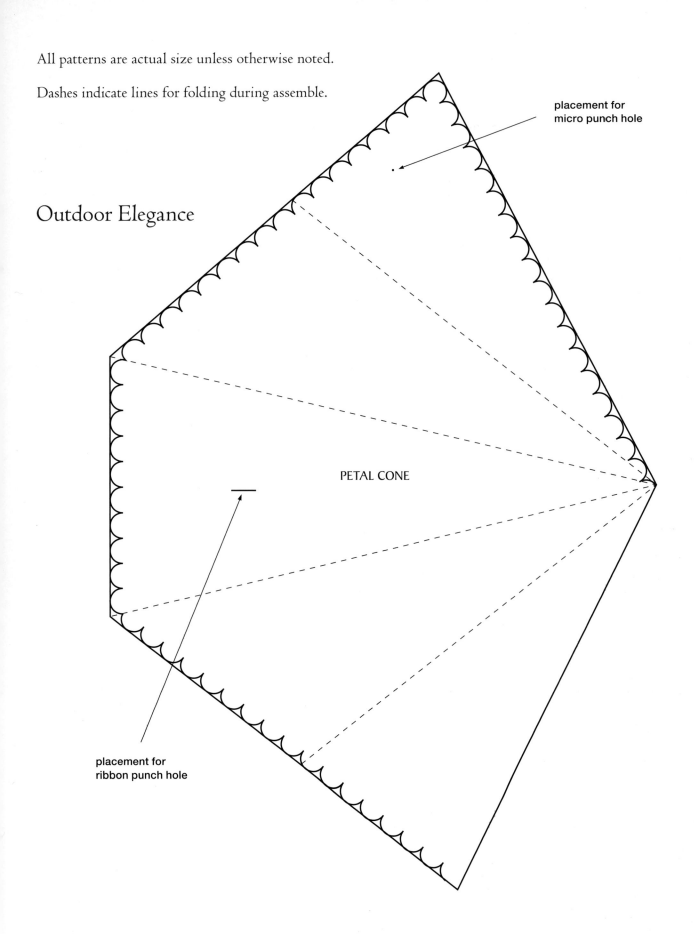

placement for
micro punch hole

Outdoor Elegance

PETAL CONE

placement for
ribbon punch hole

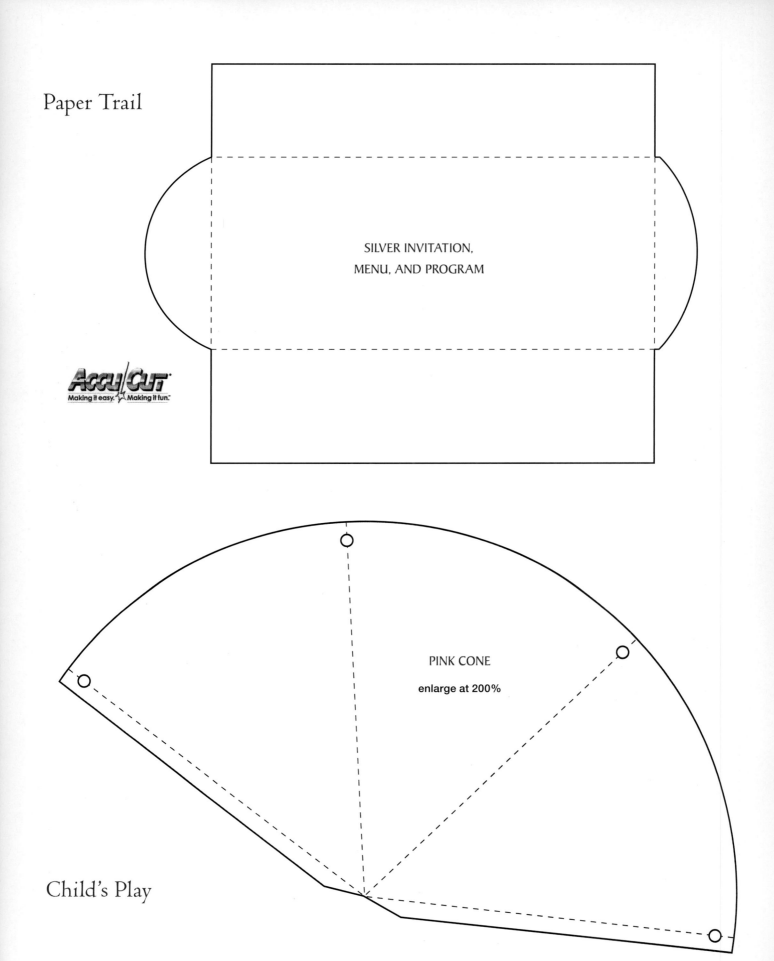

Paper Trail

SILVER INVITATION,
MENU, AND PROGRAM

PINK CONE

enlarge at 200%

Child's Play

CAKE TOP

Custom Keepsakes

CAKE CENTER

KEEPSAKE HEART

enlarge at 200%

small heart cutting line

Take the Cake *(cake under canopy)*

CAKE BOTTOM

Custom Keepsakes

CAKE-SLICE FAVOR WHEEL

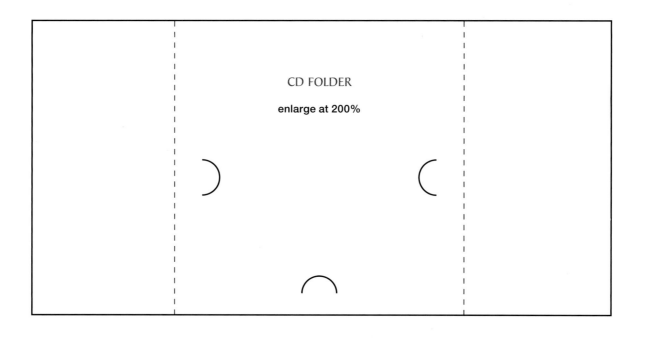

CD FOLDER

enlarge at 200%

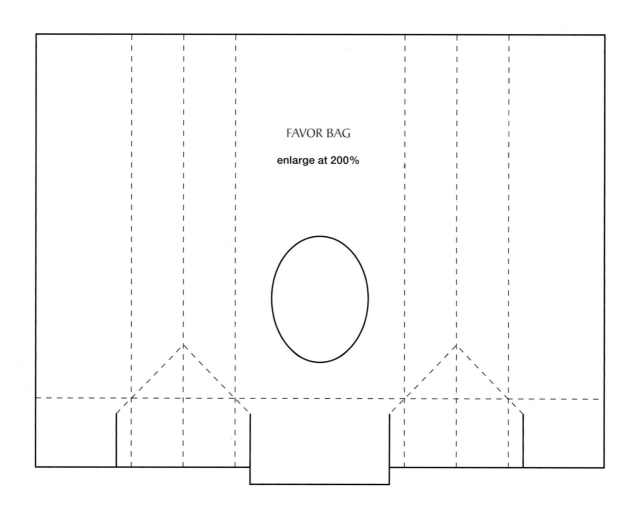

FAVOR BAG

enlarge at 200%

Better Homes and Gardens® Creative Collection®

Editorial Director John Riha

Editor in Chief Deborah Gore Ohrn

Executive Editor Karman Wittry Hotchkiss

Managing Editor Kathleen Armentrout

Contributing Editorial Manager Heidi Palkovic

Contributing Design Director Tracy DeVenney

Contributing Editor Becky Mollenkamp

Contributing Designer Maureen Miller

Copy Chief Mary Heaton
Contributing Copy Editor Jennifer Horejsi
Proofreader Joleen Ross
Administrative Assistant Lori Eggers

Publishing Group President
Jack Griffin

President and CEO Stephen M. Lacy

Chairman of the Board William T. Kerr

In Memoriam
E. T. Meredith III (1933–2003)

Contributors

Contributing Cake Designers
Cecile Gady: pages 65 (bottom left), 66 (top and bottom right), 67, 69 (bottom); **Susan Morgan:** page 66 (left); **DiAnn Neumayer:** pages 64, 65 (top left), 68 (top and bottom right); **Jennifer Peterson:** page 68 (left).

Contributing Food Stylists
Lesley Clark: pages 74–75; **Susan Devaty:** page 69 (top left and right); **Janet Pittman:** pages 64, 65 (top left), 68 (left), 72–73, 76–77; **Ray Varella:** page 66 (left).

Contributing Photographers
King Au: pages 22–27, 31 (left), 39, 49 (right), 53 (top right); **Kim Cornelison:** pages 40, 44–45, 53 (top center and bottom right), 62, 68 (left), 76–77; **Scott Little:** page 38; **Andy Lyons:** page 65 (right); **Alison Miksch and Catherine Montalbano:** pages 4–9, 30; **Greg Scheidemann:** front cover, pages 10–15, 37 (left), 41–42, 43 (top left), 49 (bottom left), 50, 51 (bottom right), 53 (top left), 55 (top and bottom right), 57, 58–59, 60 (top left), 63 (left), 64, 65 (top left), 68 (top and bottom right), 70–73; **Christina Schmidhofer:** pages 1, 16–21, 32–33, 34 (top and bottom left), 35–36, 37 (right), 43 (top right, bottom left, and bottom right), 46–48, 49 (top left), 51 (left and top right), 52, 53 (center right), 54, 55 (top left), 56

(inset), 61, 63 (top and bottom right), 65 (bottom left), 66–67, 69, 74–75; **John Schnack:** page 34 (right); **Shaun Sullivan:** page 56 (right); **Dean Tanner:** page 31 (right).

Contributing Project Designers
Karen Axel: pages 33, 34 (top and bottom left), 35–36, 37 (right); **Libby Becker and Breaca Lozier:** pages 40, 41 (bottom right), 42, 53 (top center and bottom right), 60 (bottom right), 62, 64, 65 (top left), 68 (left); **Dan Brabec:** page 38; **Scott Corridan:** pages 68 (top and bottom right), 70; **Christi Crocker:** page 56 (inset); **Dee Foust:** pages 1, 16–21, 32–33, 34 (top and bottom left), 35–36, 37 (right), 43 (top right and bottom left and right), 51 (left), 65 (bottom left), 66 (top and bottom right), 67, 69 (bottom); **Veronica Lorson Fowler:** page 39; **Lori Hellander:** front cover, pages 41 (top left), 49 (bottom left), 50 (left), 53 (top left), 55 (top and bottom right), 58–60; **Aaron Hom and Joseph Boehm:** page 56 (right); **Cathy Kramer:** page 71; **Amina Maréchal:** page 34 (right); **Saley Nong:** pages 51 (bottom right), 57, 63 (left); **Lauren Powell:** pages 37 (left), 41 (top right), 43 (top left); **Sasha Souza:** pages 46–48, 50 (top left), 54, 55 (top left); **Wanda Ventling:** pages 10–15, 22–27, 31 (left), 44–45, 49 (right), 50 (right), 53 (top right), 60 (bottom left); **Brenda Walton:** page 61.